MICHAEL DUMMETT

THE NATURE
AND FUTURE OF PHILOSOPHY

COLUMBIA UNIVERSITY PRESS ■ NEW YORK

COLUMBIA UNIVERSITY PRESS

Publishers Since 1893

New York   Chichester, West Sussex

Copyright © 2010 Michael Dummett

The Nature and Future of Philosophy was first published
in Italian translation in 2001 by Il Nuovo Melangolo

Copyright © 2001 Il Nuovo Melangolo

All rights reserved

Library of Congress Cataloging-in-Publication Data

Dummett, Michael A. E.

The nature and future of philosophy / Michael Dummett.

p.   cm. — (Columbia themes in philosophy)

ISBN 978-0-231-15052-1 (cloth : alk. paper) —
ISBN 978-0-231-15053-8 (pbk.) — ISBN 978-0-231-52218-2 (electronic)

1. Philosophy. I. Title. II. Series.

B1626.D853N3813   2010

101—dc22

2009025164

♾

Columbia University Press books are printed on permanent
and durable acid-free paper.

This book was printed on paper with recycled content.

Printed in the United States of America

c 10 9 8 7 6 5 4 3 2

p 10 9 8 7 6 5 4 3

References to Internet Web sites (URLs) were accurate at the time of writing.
Neither the author nor Columbia University Press is responsible for URLs
that may have expired or changed since the manuscript was prepared.

THE NATURE
AND FUTURE OF PHILOSOPHY

COLUMBIA THEMES IN PHILOSOPHY

COLUMBIA THEMES IN PHILOSOPHY

Editor: **Akeel Bilgrami**, Johnsonian Professor of Philosophy, Columbia University

Columbia Themes in Philosophy is a new series with a broad and accommodating thematic reach as well as an ecumenical approach to the outdated disjunction between analytical and European philosophy. It is committed to an examination of key themes in new and startling ways and to the exploration of new topics in philosophy.

Edward Said, *Humanism and Democratic Criticism*
Michael Dummett, *Truth and the Past*
John Searle, *Freedom and Neurobiology: Reflections on Free Will, Language, and Political Power*
Daniel Herwitz and Michael Kelly, eds., *Action, Art, History: Engagements with Arthur C. Danto*

CONTENTS

1

Philosophy as an Academic Subject 1

2

What Is a Philosophical Question? 7

3

Philosophy as the Grammar of Thought 13

4

Science 21

5

Psychology and Scientism 31

6

Religion and Philosophy 39

7

Religion and Morality 47

8

The Influence of Gottlob Frege 57

9

Frege's Analysis of Sentences 65

CONTENTS

10

Frege's Theory of Meaning 75

11

Gadamer on Language 87

12

The Paradox of Analysis 101

13

Thought and Language 115

14

Realism 125

15

Relativism 137

16

The Future of Philosophy 145

1

PHILOSOPHY AS
AN ACADEMIC SUBJECT

Practically every university throughout the world
deems it as essential to have a philosophy department as to have a history department or a chemistry
department. This is certainly a very lucky thing for
philosophers. Historians can teach in schools and
advise on television programs and films; the minor-
ity gifted with the ability to write popular books can
subsist on their incomes as authors. Chemists can
work for industry; if they are lucky, they may even
be paid by their companies to do research. By contrast, only in a few countries is philosophy taught as
a subject in the schools; philosophy books will never
become best-sellers; no commercial enterprise will
pay for original work in this field. Until recently,
professional philosophers would have been unem-
ployable had it not been for the universities. Some
who specialize in ethics have obtained positions
advising on bioethics, that is, on moral problems
arising out of or within the practice of medicine;
but of course this is an application of only one specialized branch of the subject. In the modern world,
scarcely anyone can live without being employed or
profitably self-employed. Philosophers not engaged

in applied ethics must count themselves extremely fortunate that the state, which funds many of the universities, is willing to pay that they may devote themselves to the pursuit of their subject.

It is by no means obvious that universities, and thus ultimately the state, should support philosophy but for historical precedent. If universities had been an invention of the second half of the twentieth century, would anyone have thought to include philosophy among the subjects that they taught and studied? It seems very doubtful. But the history of Western universities goes back 900 years—that of Islamic universities even further—and philosophy has always been one of the subjects taught and studied in them. It just does not occur to anyone not to include a philosophy department among those composing a university.

It would be easy to conclude that this is an anachronism. When the first Western universities came into being, intellectual pursuits were classified differently. Philosophy was not sharply differentiated from what we call "natural science": indeed, Oxford still has a Chair of Experimental Philosophy, which would nowadays be called a Chair of Physics. Aristotle drew no firm line between physics and metaphysics, and despite the advance of natural science from the beginning of the seventeenth century onward, the same general attitude persisted well into the eighteenth century. For the Greeks, and for almost everyone else before the nineteenth century, the quest for truth was a single activity, contrasted with the arts and the practical skills such as that of healing, but not differentiated into several diverse lines of inquiry. Different topics required different techniques and different sources of data, but there was no large-scale classification of intellectual disciplines into the sciences and the humanities. Not only for Aristotle, but still for Galileo—indeed for Einstein—physics required reasoning as well as observation and experiment, and so did not appear markedly different from those speculations based on ratiocination alone.

It was only very gradually that the experimental method came to be seen as marking a radical difference between one mode of theoretical inquiry and another. Indeed, even after the distinction between the natural sciences and the humanities came to be universally recognized, the principle of distinction has not been consistently applied. Mathematics is almost always classified with the natural sciences, under the general head of Science; but it is patently not one of the natural sciences. Its epistemic base is rationalist, not empiricist: there are no mathematical laboratories, no mathematical instruments (if we except the slide rule), no mathematical observations, no mathematical predictions the falsification of which will overturn a mathematical theory. It is classified with the natural sciences because the natural sciences (like some of the social sciences, such as economics) make extensive use of it and to a great extent formulate their theories in its terms. But, however useful it may be to the sciences, in its intrinsic nature it is something very different from them.

Furthermore, even after the distinction between philosophy and the natural sciences came to be generally admitted, the ground of differentiation between philosophy and science still did not guide the boundary lines drawn around the discipline of philosophy. Psychology, as a scientific discipline, was born in the nineteenth century within the philosophy departments of universities; after all, psychology, pursued by rational methods alone, was already solidly established as a branch of philosophy. Only gradually did experimental psychology disentangle itself from philosophy. And the process has continued: philosophy has budded off yet other subjects that have declared their independence from it. Logic was formerly regarded as a branch of philosophy, but with the new logic of Frege, Peano, Russell, and Hilbert, it defined itself as mathematical logic and sought a home within mathematics, which was not at first very eager to welcome it. General linguistics, likewise, parted company with philosophy, which had nurtured it, and largely took over the independent subject of philology. In yet more recent times, cognitive science has raided philosophical territory and set itself up as a science in its own right.

No practicing philosopher would explain the value of the subject merely as a matrix out of which new disciplines could develop. But what is it? What is left when the disciplines to which it gave birth have left the parental home? What remains is a discipline that makes no observations, conducts no experiments, and needs no input from experience: an armchair subject, requiring only thought. An empiricist outlook induces skepticism about whether there can be such a subject: surely all knowledge derives from experience. A ready retort would be to ask, "What experience gives you that piece of knowledge?" but the retort would probably not impress the skeptic. What does impress him is the existence and success of another armchair discipline: mathematics. Mathematics likewise needs no input from experience: it is the product of thought alone. Its achievements would be astonishing even if it were of no use, but it is dubious whether those achievements, rather than its uses, guaranteed that it should continue to be an integral ingredient of university studies. Some mathematicians disdain the applications of mathematics: G. H. Hardy rejoiced in the thought that nothing he had ever accomplished in the subject could be of any use to nonmathematicians. This, however, has by no means been the attitude of philosophers of mathematics. Frege, whose own work in mathematics was highly abstract, wrote that "It is applicability alone that raises arithmetic from the rank of a game to that of a science"; he included analysis—the theory of real and complex numbers—under "arithmetic" and did not mean by "a science" one of the "natural sciences," but simply "a sector in the systematic quest for truth." Whether he was right or not to say this, it is the fact that mathematics is essential to science that makes it an indispensable component of university research and teaching.

The example of mathematics benefits philosophy, despite their very different methodologies, by proving that thought, without any specialized input from experience, can advance knowledge in unexpected directions. But mathematics shares with philosophy a difficulty in saying what it is *about*. Mathematicians do not concern themselves to find any general answer to this question: it is for philosophers to say not only what, in general, philosophy is about, but also what, in general, mathematics is about.

2

WHAT IS A PHILOSOPHICAL QUESTION?

What, then, is philosophy about? For Quine and some other contemporary American philosophers, philosophy is simply the most abstract part of science. It does not, indeed, make any observations or conduct any experiments of its own; but it may, and should, incorporate the discoveries of the sciences to build a naturalized theory of knowledge and of the mind. Properly speaking, therefore, it ought to be classified with the natural sciences. Wittgenstein held the very opposite opinion. For him, philosophy stands in complete contrast with science: its methods wholly diverge from those of science, and its objective differs to an equal extent. Probably most philosophers practicing today would agree with this, and would add that the results of philosophy differ fundamentally in character from those of the sciences. Wittgenstein was more radical. He did not think that philosophy has any results, in the form of statable propositions it has discovered to be true; philosophy merely casts light on what we already know from other sources, enabling us to see it with eyes unclouded by intellectual confusion.

The best way to judge this disagreement, and say what philosophy is about and by what means it proceeds, is to contemplate a sample philosophical problem. For the reasons explained in the preceding chapter, it was not until the nineteenth century that it made sense to ask for an example of a philosophical problem, as opposed to a problem of some other kind; even now there could easily be disputes over whether one or another particular problem was genuinely a philosophical one or not. But there are paradigm cases of problems that everyone would agree are philosophical in character. One is this: Does time really pass? Some may say that it evidently does: the world changes as new events occur; these events formerly lay in the future, and will in due time be over and recede into the past. But some deny that time passes in this sense. There are temporal relations between events—certain events temporally precede others—but this is all there is to time: its being a dimension on which events have different locations.

This is plainly a philosophical disagreement. It is indeed a metaphysical disagreement: it concerns the nature, not of the human mind or human behavior, but of external reality. Faced with such a disagreement, how does a philosopher proceed? He may begin by asking the believers in the passage of time to clarify their view. What, he may ask, do they think that there is? Some may reply that what is yet to be *is* not, and that what has ceased to be *is* not: all there *is* is what exists now. Does this mean, he inquires, that statements about what will happen or about how things formerly were are neither true nor false? For, he urges, a statement can be true only if there is something in virtue of which it is true: so, if all there is is what exists now, no statement about the future or about the past can be true. Some may enthusiastically agree. Reality, they say, is ever-changing. The only true statements are those that represent reality as it is, that is, as it is *now*; there can be no truths about how it will be or how it was.

Other believers in the passage of time may give a more temperate response. They may urge that the philosopher is forgetting that the verb "to be" has tenses. If it be asked what there is, in the present tense, the answer must be restricted to the present moment; but there are also answers to the questions of what there will be and what there has been. The principle that a statement can be true only if there is something in virtue of which it is true overlooks the tensed nature of the verb "to be": it should be "true only if there is, will be, or has been something in virtue of which it is true." What, then, differentiates such a view from that of those who deny the passage of time? the philosopher asks. Those people leave out of their description of reality an essential fact, he is told, namely, that certain of the events ordered by temporal sequence are occurring *now*.

The skeptic replies that the question "Which event is happening now?" merely asks which event is simultaneous with the asking of the question, which is itself just another event. No, his opponent answers. When a painful experience has ceased and I exclaim, "Thank God that's over," I am not rejoicing in a mere relation of temporal precedence, he says, for I knew in advance that I should say, "Thank God that's over," and that my saying it would take place only after the experience had come to an end. All that means, the opponent of temporal passage retorts, is that your feeling of relief followed, rather than preceded, the end of the painful experience: it is still just a matter of temporal sequence.

The believer in the passage of time may now object that his opponent is spatializing time, treating it as just one more dimension in addition to the three of space. That, he says, abolishes time, since it does not allow the reality of changes, whereas change is of the essence of time. His opponent replies that he does recognize change: there is change whenever a true proposition is converted into a false one by replacing some temporal specification occurring in it with a different one. "That's just what I mean," the defender of the passage of time may exclaim: "you could define 'spatial change' by substituting 'specification of place' for 'temporal specification'; but the fact that there is grass at this place and none a kilometer away does not involve that any change has occurred or is occurring." "That is contrary to the way we talk," it may be retorted; we say such things as "The terrain changes to the east of the spot." "Only because we imagine ourselves traveling in that direction," the other replies.

We need not follow the debate over this well-known philosophical dispute any further; taken only so far, it adequately illustrates the character of the philosophical argument. The dispute certainly concerns reality: according to the view anyone takes concerning it, he will conceive of the world in one way or the other. But the matter is not one to be settled by empirical means: scientific theory may bear on it—for example, it is relevant that, according to special relativity, simultaneity is relative to a frame of reference. But science could not resolve the dispute: no observation could establish that one or the other side was right. A philosopher will seek either to show that one of the disputants is right and the other wrong, perhaps after some further clarification of the two views, or else to dissolve the dispute by showing both sides to be victims of some conceptual confusion. Philosophy is indeed concerned with reality, but not to discover new facts about it: it seeks to improve our understanding of what we already know. It does not seek to observe more, but to clarify our vision of what we see. Its aim is, in Wittgenstein's phrase, to help us to see the world aright.

Whether the philosopher claims to have solved a problem or to have dissolved it as a pseudo-problem, he will proceed by rational argument. Philosophy shares with mathematics the peculiarity that it does not appeal to any new sources of information, but relies solely upon reasoning on the basis of what we already know. It differs from mathematics in that it prefers muddy territory. Mathematicians have sometimes to engage in conceptual analysis, seeking definitions of concepts such as numerical equivalence, continuity, and dimension. But their aims differ from those of philosophers. They care little whether the definitions they arrive at capture the concept as we implicitly understand it in ordinary life: they are concerned only to formulate a precise concept under which it may be reasonably claimed that every case determinately either falls or does not fall. Having done so, their argumentation will proceed within the boundaries of the definitions they have adopted. The philosopher's reasoning takes place on the basis of our existing implicit understanding; it appeals to that understanding and hence is not carried out, as the mathematician's is, within a framework of concepts already made precise.

Thus the philosopher's only resource is the analysis of concepts we already possess, but about which we are confused; he seeks to remove that confusion. Whether he strives to do so by an analysis of expressions of our language or by some other means is a matter of his philosophical methodology; methodological differences may be sharp, but the aim is the same. In the sample philosophical dispute we examined, the philosopher cannot argue on the basis of the primitive apprehension of temporal succession that may be attributed to an infant. The question that was at issue can arise only for an adult to whom our ways of speaking about time in language are known. It is thus sterile to ask whether philosophy is about reality, about the concepts in terms of which we think about reality, or about the linguistic means we use to express those concepts. It concerns our view of reality by seeking to clarify the concepts in terms of which we conceive of it, and hence the linguistic expressions by means of which we formulate our conception.

3

PHILOSOPHY AS THE
GRAMMAR OF THOUGHT

That the task of philosophy is to clarify our concepts does not entail that there are no philosophical truths, no statements that embody the results of philosophical clarification. Wittgenstein's own work belies his denial that philosophical endeavor can be encapsulated in propositions. Many arguments of his drive toward conclusions expressible as philosophical theses. A clear example is his celebrated reflections on the notion of a private language—a language private in the sense that only one person could understand it—which lead to the conclusion that there could not be a private language: a clear example of a philosophical thesis with strong consequences for the untenability of various conceptions that have tempted many thinkers into accepting and propounding them. This is only one of numerous counterexamples, derivable from Wittgenstein's own work, to his denial that philosophy has any results expressible as propositions.

Such philosophical theses have, however, a quite special character: they are what Wittgenstein himself called "grammatical remarks." That is to say, they are not properly regarded as telling us how the world is, but rather as guiding us to recognize what does and does not make sense to say, and hence what may and may not intelligibly be thought. It is for this reason that they frequently have a modal form, laying down what must be so and what cannot be so. The necessity is conceptual necessity: this or that must be so because to describe anything otherwise would involve contradiction or conceptual confusion. When the question concerns the underlying logical form of some class of propositions, the answer is almost literally grammatical. Scholastic logicians had great trouble explaining the difference in significance of the words expressed in English by "any" and "every." That philosophy does make progress, and even achieves assured results, is shown by the fact that what perplexed medieval logicians is now a five-finger exercise for beginners. Nowadays any beginning student in formal logic would be able to explain the distinction between "You may come any day next week" and "You may come every day next week" by analyzing the first as "For every day d next week, it is permitted that you come on d" and the second as "It is permitted that, for every day d next week, you come on d." This exemplifies the process described by Quine as "regimenting" sentences of natural language.

It is open to dispute what the process of regimentation consists in. It is clearly an exercise in semantics, where a semantic theory explains how the condition for the truth or falsity of a sentence is determined in accordance with the composition of the sentence from its component words. The most modest description would be that it is a process by means of which a sentence of natural language of which it is difficult to give a semantic account is replaced by a (stylistically clumsy) sentence of natural language, supplemented by variable letters, for which we can give a straightforward semantic account: the regimented form expresses just the same thought as the original colloquial form. A more grandiose claim is that the regimented sentence displays the structure of the thought expressed by the colloquial sentence. A linguist may claim that the regimented version represents the deep structure of the sentence, transformed unconsciously by a competent speaker in accordance with general rules into the surface form actually uttered. However the process of regimentation is interpreted, it yields a clear means of specifying the contrasting meanings of "any" and "every."

Just as grammatical in an all but literal sense are disputed proposals for analyzing the logical form of sentences of one or another class, for example, that of Donald Davidson for explaining the operation of adverbs and adverbial phrases of a familiar type. Some adverbs, such as "probably," "supposedly," and so on, modify the entire clause in which they figure, and with these Davidson was not concerned. Others, such as "quickly," "patiently," "on Wednesday," "with a fork," and so on, modify the predicate, and it was these that Davidson sought to explain. His theory is that a narrative sentence—one reporting an event or action—should be understood as having a tacit existential quantifier binding a variable ranging over events. The verb and the grammatical subject and object of the sentence are in effect predicates attached to this variable, specifying the type of event, the agent (animate or inanimate), and the subject of the event or action, and the adverbs and adverbial phrases are likewise predicates attached to it, all connected by conjunction. The point of this analysis is to explain two features of such sentences: first, how it is that any such sentence entails the sentence that results from deleting any adverb or adverbial phrase; and second, the fact that there is no limit on the number of adverbs or adverbial phrases that may arrive at a more detailed description of what happened. Davidson's theory is obviously a great improvement on the theory that the predicate of an action sentence contains a large number of tacit argument places—for the time of the event, its place, its manner, and so forth—governed, when not filled explicitly, by a sequence of existential quantifiers. The form of semantic theory we understand very well is that which governs a language expressed by sentences exemplifying schemas of first-order (quantificational) predicate logic, which allows no place for adverbs as such. Davidson's proposal—like the inferior one to which it is to be preferred—offers a means of expressing action sentences in just such a language. It does not rest upon any thesis that the only clear semantic theory we can devise is that which governs sentences fashioned after the model of first-order predicate logic. A rival theory of action sentences proposing an analysis that diverges from that model could just as well be entertained, provided that it was accompanied by a semantic theory, as clear as what we have for predicate logic, governing sentences of the form envisaged in that analysis. Davidson's analysis regiments action sentences in the framework of predicate logic, governed by a known semantic theory, but with no presumption that that was the only possible framework for analyzing them.

Philosophers of the analytic school accept without cavil that theses about the logical form of sentences or other linguistic expressions are among the proper concerns of philosophy. Those of the type generally termed "continental" usually have little interest in them, because although they may extol language, as in Hans-Georg Gadamer's celebrated declaration that "The Being that can be understood is language" (*Truth and Method*, English translation of *Wahrheit und Methode* [London: 1975 and 1979], 432), they do not seek to analyze it or explain its workings.

Indeed, the term "language" in Gadamer's epigram is being used in an extended sense, to cover everything of human invention about which it makes sense to say that it is to be understood, and hence that, in a very general sense, it has meaning. Among the things that are thus for Gadamer objects of understanding are works of art. Language, in Gadamer's sense, is whatever may be a vehicle of communication, that is, of the expression of meaning in the extended sense. He is even disposed to apply the concepts of truth to works of art and to everything that calls, in this sense, for understanding. There undoubtedly is a legitimate extension of the notions of understanding and of meaning from the realm of propositions to the much broader realm that interests Gadamer. From the standpoint of philosophers working in the tradition of Frege, however—that is, of analytic philosophers—to concentrate on understanding in this broader sense is a mistake. A painting or a piece of music affects our sensibility. It may alter our attitudes, often profoundly, or enrich our emotions; it may even bring us to recognize as true what we had previously dismissed, but it does not of itself convey knowledge. Knowledge consists in the apprehension of the truth of propositions, and propositions can be communicated only by means of language. It is therefore only through the analysis of linguistic meaning that we can attain an insight into the structure of our thought. The structure of thought is the primary concern of philosophy, since it is in thought that we apprehend reality.

It may be urged on behalf of the "continental" view that questions concerning logical form do not belong to philosophy, properly so called: they are questions of logic, and logic, on this view, is only historically conceived as part of philosophy. Although questions about logical form do not interest the general public, which wants philosophy to address more far-reaching questions, this is a narrow-sighted view. If philosophy is concerned with analyzing the concepts in terms of which we think, it needs as a basis a conspectus of how our words combine to yield meaningful sentences, and thus how our concepts hang together to form full-fledged thoughts. A theory of how the meanings of sentences are derived from their composition—a semantic theory—can often have resounding consequences for metaphysical questions: questions concerning the nature of reality depend heavily on the answers to questions about how we can speak about reality, and thus on the structure of our thought about it. I myself believe, and have argued, that disputes for and against realistic interpretations of various ranges of propositions turn eventually on the general form of a semantic analysis of the propositions.

Davidson's theory of adverbs, which may at first appear metaphysically sterile, is a case in point. We speak of objects of a variety of kinds, and classify them, by means of common nouns, as stars, trees, cats, cities, mountains, human beings, and so on; and of course we use proper names for objects of all these kinds. We likewise speak of events of a variety of kinds, and classify them, by means of common nouns, as earthquakes, weddings, battles, encounters, volcanic eruptions, banquets, and the like; and we use proper names for some of them and complex singular terms for others. But it has often been maintained that we do not need to recognize events as among the things there are: in old-fashioned metaphysical terminology, they are not among the ultimate constituents of reality; in more modern jargon, we ought not to admit them into our ontology. The ground given for this contention is that we could express all that we want to say without using either general or singular terms for events, only narrative sentences. If Davidson's analysis of narrative sentences is correct, such an argument is fallacious. On Davidson's theory, each narrative sentence should be understood as tacitly involving quantification over events: and we can quantify over things of a given kind only if we presuppose that there are things of that kind.

Wittgenstein's epithet "grammatical" did not apply to such analyses of the logical form of sentences; he was not interested, and perhaps did not believe, in semantic theories. By a "grammatical proposition" he meant one serving to indicate what it does and does not make sense to say. A very simple example is the proposition that only I can feel my pain: this rules out any intelligible use of an expression of such a form as "Margaret felt in her shoulder the pain of the wound in George's shoulder." What purports to be a proposition embodying the conclusion of a philosophical argument must, on Wittgenstein's view, always be aimed at being grammatical in this sense.

This is not easy to maintain: propositions such as that time really passes, or that vagueness is a feature of language and not of reality, may bear indirectly on what it makes sense to say; but they certainly cannot be directly interpreted as excluding particular forms of expression as illegitimate or nonsensical. Nevertheless, though they may not be propositions about the grammar of linguistic expressions in even the broadest sense, they patently seek to encapsulate attempts to clarify concepts—the concept of time or the concept of vagueness respectively; they are headings for some endeavor, successful or unsuccessful, to unravel intellectual confusions to which we are readily subject. Concepts are to complete thoughts, roughly speaking, as words are to sentences; and so we may say, in a phrase that Wittgenstein would greatly have disliked, that philosophical propositions are contributions to the grammar of thought and so, indirectly, to the grammar of the language in which we express our thoughts.

4

SCIENCE

On the view of philosophy argued for in the preceding chapters, philosophy does not advance knowledge: it clarifies what we already know. This clarification will affect our understanding of reality; it will dispel the misunderstandings and confusions that distort our thinking about it. To arrive at the goal at which philosophy aims is to follow a tortuous path. There are so many problems to which we do not know the solution: the relation of mind and body, the sense in which our actions are free, the ground of morality, the nature of time. What is consciousness, and could we behave just as we did without it? Is consciousness possible only for living organisms, or can there be unembodied minds? Does it make sense to believe in existence after death without the body? Would a complete description of physical events incorporate all that there is in the universe, or would it leave some things out? On what presuppositions does the idea rest that someone may *deserve* good or bad things happening to him, and are we entitled to these presuppositions? Are moral values to be discerned within the natural world, including the world of human behavior, or do they derive from some other sector of reality? All these, and many questions besides, are proper to philosophy. To several of them a large majority of philosophers would reply in the same way, but would be unable to claim any definitive, unchallengeable demonstration that their answers were correct. Many others remain highly contested topics. Many philosophers have solutions that satisfy them, but must acknowledge that these solutions are not accepted, or not properly understood, by the majority of other philosophers.

Philosophical progress unquestionably occurs, but it is exceedingly slow. The progress consists in establishing that certain lines of argument fail, showing how they can be strengthened, drawing previously unperceived distinctions. By such means philosophy inches along a winding path. The path constantly twists back on itself, so the direction it faces at any one stage is a virtually worthless clue to the direction in which the eventual solution lies; but, as in a maze, the only way of reaching the center—the eventual solution to or dissolution of the problem—is to advance along that twisting path.

It is not only the slow pace at which philosophy arrives at agreed results that, at first sight, diminishes its contribution to understanding the world. Even a wholehearted disciple of a philosopher who offers plausible solutions to all the foregoing problems must concede that, in a certain respect, science has contributed far more to our conception of the universe than philosophy has done. Science has immensely enlarged the spatial and temporal boundaries of the world. It has given us knowledge of the ages of the human race, of life on our planet, of the earth itself, of the solar system, of the galaxy, and even of the universe as a whole. Even if these estimates have later to be revised, we have derived from them a conception of the scale of the whole process of creation that has utterly overthrown what was believed when Saint Augustine dismissed as a product of the vain pride of human kingdoms the Egyptian chronology that went back to before what he supposed the Bible taught was the age of the universe. Science has likewise taught us the vast extent of the physical universe—around 10^{11} galaxies each containing around 10^{11} stars. How shrunken the Ptolemaic universe is in comparison to what we know of the real one.

The Ptolemaic system was of course first overthrown by the genius of Copernicus and of his great successor Galileo. Shocking as the overthrow originally appeared to many, the heliocentric model was no more than a minor adjustment, but it opened the way to the several steps that have taken us to the realization that we inhabit, not the center of the cosmos, but a small satellite of a middle-sized star in a conglomeration of a hundred thousand million stars, which in turn is only one of a hundred thousand million such conglomerations. This realization may both stagger and terrify us but does not affront common sense. It is neither rational nor natural to assume that the sun goes around the earth, simply thoughtless. The assumption should be countered by Wittgenstein's question, "How would it look if it looked as though the earth rotated on its axis?"

The evolution of species, though now, so long after Darwin, such a familiar idea, does affront common sense. Everyday observation would naturally suggest a steady-state theory of life on earth. Everyday observation assures us that you cannot get an oak save from an acorn, or a horse save from a mare impregnated by a stallion; the natural conclusion is that the fauna and flora of the earth have always been much as they are now. (The success of human beings in breeding new varieties of domesticated species in no way suggests that new species may have come into existence without human interference.)

It is perhaps a slightly puzzling thing that no people has ever interpreted "always" in "always much as now" as meaning "throughout infinite past time": even Hindu mythology attributes a temporal beginning to the world. It appears to be a natural inclination of the human mind to suppose that everything must have had a beginning; that is what gave the beautiful steady-state theory of the universe, now abandoned, its paradoxical flavor. It may be said that the principle that everything has a beginning is derived from everyday observation, including children's early realization that they themselves have existed for only a few years. That children so easily grasp this is somewhat puzzling. It is often said that it is very hard for children to understand that they, and all around them, are destined to die; but it is not obvious that it is harder to realize that one will not always exist than that one has not always existed. Furthermore, from the fact that everything in the world has a beginning, it no way follows that the world as a whole must have had a beginning.

However this may be, "common sense" has always included the assumption that the world must have had a beginning in time; but it is equally part of common sense to suppose that it was from the beginning, and has always thereafter been, much as it is now. Nineteenth-century paleontology first exploded this natural idea, showing the variation in animal and plant forms that had populated the earth in different ages; and nineteenth-century geology first gave us a realistic conception of the age of our planet and of the enormous changes its surface has undergone. It was of course Darwin and Wallace who first supplied a sound explanation of how animal and plant species might have evolved and given way to new ones. These are ideas now commonplace for everyone but certain clusters of fanatics in the United States, but when introduced, they violated what it was not only natural but also rational to suppose.

Science has thus disclosed how the incredible diversity of species has developed from simple forms of life. More recently, it has uncovered the mechanism of heredity. It has explained to us the nature of light and other forms of radiation. It has taught us the true composition of matter out of molecules and atoms, the grounds in this composition of the behavior of the various substances that it assumes, and the extraordinary forms that matter can take on in extreme conditions. It has offered for our bewilderment the realm of the particles out of which the atoms are composed. It has revealed to us the intertwining of space and time. In short, it has provided us with a picture of reality that in large part we have come to take for granted, but that differs completely from what even quite a sophisticated inspection of the world around us would, and indeed did once, suggest. It has changed our conception of reality from what common sense presented far more radically than philosophy ever sought to do.

The far greater impact of natural science than of philosophy upon our conception of the universe does not at all imply that science is independent of philosophy. Physics, in particular, continually throws up new philosophical problems or new forms of old philosophical problems. This fact alone demonstrates the indispensability of philosophy, though not necessarily of professional philosophers: physicists and mathematicians may engage in philosophical reflection and philosophical argument. Philosophical problems generated by physics are not to be resolved by observation or by experiment, but only, like all philosophical problems, by rational reflection. A good example of a problem arising out of physics is that of the direction, or arrow, of time. It is commonplace to remark that most physical laws are symmetric with respect to the earlier-to-later direction, with the increase of entropy. But why does the second law of thermodynamics hold good? What is the ground of its temporal asymmetry? Attempts are frequently made to justify it by appeal to consideration of probability. It should be evident, however, that any such appeal must assume the arrow of time as given, and therefore cannot succeed in explaining it. Probability theory is, in itself, temporally symmetric: an asymmetry cannot be grounded on symmetry. It is true enough that, given a highly ordered state of a system, it is probable that the system will subsequently exhibit a far lesser degree of order. But, by parity of reasoning, it is equally probable that it should previously have exhibited a far lesser degree of order: no general conclusion can be drawn. The illusion of being able so to derive one is based on the assumption that the state of the system at any one time depends upon its state at previous times, not upon its state at subsequent times, and this is precisely to assume the directedness of time rather than to derive it. What, then, determines the direction of time? Is it a universal feature that characterizes the entire physical cosmos, or is it possible that it is a local phenomenon? Is the fact that we have memory but not precognition, understood as the mirror image of memory about the present as axis of reflection, simply a particular exemplification of the directedness of time? Or is it a contingent fact about us that causes us to perceive the arrow of time as flying from past to future? All these form a cluster of characteristically philosophical questions, not to be answered with assurance without a substantial knowledge of physics, but equally unamenable to being settled by experiment: no cyclotron could be built to resolve them.

A question, part technical, part philosophical, treated as pressing by very few at present, is whether physical theories are justified in relying as they do on classical mathematics. Small minorities among mathematicians, principally those of the schools of L. E. J. Brouwer and of Everett Bishop, pursue mathematics in the constructive rather than the classical style. Constructive mathematics repudiates forms of reasoning, freely admitted in classical mathematics, based on the assumption that every precisely formulated mathematical proposition is determinately either true or false, independently of our knowledge or capacity to know. Instead, it grounds the meanings of mathematical propositions on constructions that human mathematicians can actually carry out, at least in principle. It might be thought that physicists, still enwreathed in wisps of the positivism bequeathed to them by Mach and others, at least to the extent of being concerned that their physical theories be testable by experiment or observation, would be more attracted by constructive mathematics than by the classical variety, whose most natural philosophical interpretation is in terms of the reality of a platonic realm of abstract entities. Instead, they ignore or are unaware of constructive mathematics. An important question in the philosophy of physics, and in its practice as well, is whether physical theories could be based on constructive rather than classical mathematics, and if so, how great a transformation this would bring about in them; so far, this question has been very little investigated.

A particular aspect of this question is how justified is the use of the classical continuum of real numbers as a model for continuous quantities such as time, a model embodying the assumption that the magnitude of any such quantity—the duration of a temporal interval, for example—is given in reality, relative to any chosen unit such as a second, by a specific real number, a measure not of course known to us except within an approximation. The use of the classical continuum as a model is not derived from reality or from our experience of reality; it has been imposed by us upon reality, as constituting the only precise way in which we have succeeded in conceiving of continuity. But the fit of model to reality is far from good. In particular, it fails to give a good representation of change in the magnitude of a continuous quantity. The model makes the magnitude of such a quantity, relative to a given unit, a function defined on real numbers representing temporal instants with real numbers as values. Although the real line is itself continuous, such a function, considered only as defined for every real number as argument, need not be continuous. The model therefore makes the continuity of change in the magnitude of the given quantity dependent on contingent laws of physics rather than a matter of conceptual necessity, which it ought to be. It is what makes fantasies such as that of infinitely many oscillations of the same amplitude in a finite time appear physically conceivable and only precluded by contingent laws. A model based on constructive mathematics ought to overcome this awkwardness: in the so-called "intuitionistic" version of mathematics proposed by Brouwer, a function defined on all real numbers will be demonstrably continuous.

The questionable character of the classical continuum as a model for physical reality has a bearing on determinism. A system may be chaotic in that we are prevented from predicting its future because a very small variation in the initial conditions may have a large consequence for its subsequent state. The system may yet be reckoned to be deterministic because its theory requires that any precise determination of the initial conditions will yield a determinate outcome at any subsequent time. To describe it as deterministic on such a ground is to assume that the initial parameters have, in reality, precise values, given relatively to suitable units by specific real numbers, although these precise values are not ascertainable by us. If, however, it is not justifiable to assume that the initial parameters have any such precise values, then the indeterminacy of our predictions is transferred to an indeterminacy in the actual development of the system, which can no longer be called deterministic.

The outstanding example of a philosophical problem arising out of physical theory is the interpretation of quantum mechanics. Religious believers are sometimes scoffed at for believing in the truth of dogmas that they do not understand; quantum mechanics is in just this position for physicists. While they are in universal accord that the agreement of its predictions with observation guarantees the correctness of quantum mechanics as a physical theory, they are in constant dispute over its interpretation; it could be said that they are convinced of its truth but do not know what it means. The theory is regarded as correct because physicists know how to use it to predict the results of experiments, and these agree with observation; but what is it to "interpret" the theory? To propose an interpretation of quantum mechanics is to give an account of the constitution of reality that accords with that theory. This is notoriously difficult to do, and it is plainly a philosophical problem. Indeed, it may be said to have the general form of all philosophical problems. We operate well enough with our ordinary concepts for our practical purposes: we know how to employ them in our everyday affairs. But we become confused when we attempt to use them to form a coherent picture of reality. It is the task of philosophy to extricate us from this confusion.

Does light consist of waves, or is it a stream of particles? Does it make sense to reply, "Both" or "The one in certain phenomena, the other in other phenomena"? What reality corresponds to a superposition of states? Can a cat be in a superposition of death and life? If not, where does the boundary between the macroscopic and the microscopic run? Can the measurement of the spin of one particle determine that of another, too far removed for any causal influence to reach it? If so, how should the concept of causality be explained? Can a human action bring something about without causing it? These and a plethora of similar questions are aroused by quantum mechanics. What does the theory tell us about physical reality? Or ought we to abandon the idea that it tells us anything about reality, and adopt a purely instrumentalist view of quantum mechanics as merely a piece of mathematics that enables us to calculate in advance what we shall observe when we make certain experimental preparations? If we were to take this easy exit from perplexity, we could not very well refuse an instrumentalist view of all other science. Reality would then be for us only what is presented by gross observation, unsupplemented instruments, experiment, or theory. This is almost certainly an unstable stance to adopt. We must settle for trying to determine how reality must be for quantum mechanics genuinely to be a correct theory. Of course, should it be abandoned or amended, the metaphysical conclusions we had drawn from it would need to be jettisoned or themselves amended. In the meantime, we face a cluster of problems that must be tackled by the techniques of the philosopher, not of the physicist.

It is no paradox that science should throw up new puzzles for philosophy to resolve. Science and philosophy are not rivals; both are concerned to improve our picture of reality, but in quite different ways. Science supplies us with ever more facts about reality, although to do so, it has often to fashion new concepts in terms of which to state those facts. It thus enlarges our field of vision. Philosophy seeks to rectify our vision, enabling us, as Wittgenstein said, to see the world aright, including those features of the world that science reveals. It does so by the slow, laborious process of clarifying our concepts, both our everyday concepts and the new concepts introduced by science. The two are complementary: both are engaged in mankind's long quest for truth.

5

PSYCHOLOGY AND SCIENTISM

The astounding advances made during the past half-millennium by physics, astronomy, and cosmology have radically altered our picture of the universe, but they have had very little effect upon our understanding of ourselves and of our dealings with one another. Even the success of biology in establishing the evolution of species, including our own, and explaining its mechanism in natural selection has done comparatively little to alter our view of human beings and the relations between them. The technology born of science has indeed utterly transformed our lives: it has given us swift means of travel, rapid communication across great distances, easy access to information, greatly improved medical relief of injury and disease, and anaesthetics to protect us from the pain of surgical operations; it has also given us horrifying means of mass destruction to be used in warfare. None of this, however, affects our conception of ourselves and of human society. A large sector of philosophy—all that falls under the head of metaphysics—is constrained to take account of the discoveries of physics and cosmology, just as the philosophy of mathematics must take account of the advances of mathematical logic. In the same way, the philosophy of perception has to take account of the results of experimental psychology. Other sectors of philosophy—ethics, political philosophy, and those parts of the philosophy of mind that relate not to sense perception but to such concepts as intention, motive, and emotion—can at present still be pursued in much the same way as before, without any great need to pay attention to scientific data.

Among the general public, biology has begun to have an impact on ordinary modes of thought. Evolutionary explanations of human behavior—for instance, attempted demonstrations of the evolutionary advantage to a species of altruistic behavior on the part of its members—have not much affected the moral thinking of ordinary people. Quite rightly, no one considers what he ought to do in any situation in terms of its propensity to favor the survival of genes resembling his own. But the notion of the gene has entered the general consciousness and given rise to absurd speculations about whether there can be a gene for this or that character trait. Science knows as yet far too little about the genetic makeup of human beings, or of any other species, to provide substance for any such speculations; their effect is simply to make everyone more prone than before to attribute features of the behavior of individuals to their heredity rather than to their upbringing or their personal choice. The neurological study of the functioning of the brain has had a more far-reaching effect upon common thinking. We are more aware than we once were of the effect, often catastrophic, on our mental faculties of damage to the brain; we regard that organ less as the instrument of the mind than as its seat.

This tendency is also prevalent among American philosophers and many British ones. A few of the former—notably Jerry Fodor—have been deeply influenced by the psychologists and have fashioned philosophical theories, such as Fodor's notion of the "language of thought," on the model of ideas prevalent among practitioners of experimental psychology. More generally, analytic philosophers have become prone to speak of the brain rather than of the mind, and of theses in the philosophy of mind as, in effect, high-level propositions about the organization of the brain. Most, indeed, subscribe to the theory that mental states are literally identical with states of the brain, and mental events with processes within the brain. It is highly debatable whether, in the sense in which a sound may be identified with waves of compression and rarefaction in the air, the formation of a liking for a new acquaintance could be identical with a process in the brain. Saul Kripke, deploying his notion of rigid designation, has attempted to demonstrate that this could not be so for sensations of pain. In any case, although much is now known about the operation of the brain, neurological science remains far from able to establish a correspondence between specific mental occurrences and particular events in the brain, whether the correspondence be deemed a relation of identity or only a correlation. The wish to safeguard a materialistic metaphysics, pervasive in present-day analytic philosophy, nevertheless grounds a faith that such a correspondence will eventually be established, and that even if it is not, identity between mental states and events, and states and events in the brain, must hold good, discoverable or otherwise.

A small number of analytic philosophers—notoriously the two Churchlands—treat the absence of any detailed correspondence as an objection not to the thesis of mind/brain identity, but to reliance on our familiar mental concepts. The use of concepts such as desire, purpose, remembering and forgetting, ambition, belief, and so forth is scoffed at as "folk psychology." When the twin sciences of neurology and psychology have sufficiently progressed, this system of "folk" concepts will, we are assured, be replaced by a wholly new system of properly scientific concepts. Given that no such new system is yet available, one might think that the best strategy for anyone convinced that it will at some time be devised would be to abandon this area of philosophy until then.

A different response, that of Davidson, is to deny that any correspondence between type of mental events and a specific type of brain process is ever to be expected. Davidson has argued, on grounds to do with causality, that each particular mental event must be literally identical with some brain process, but that no match can ever be established, or can exist, between any one *type* of mental event—say, suffering a pang of remorse—and any corresponding *type* of process in the brain, not even for some one individual. The materialism remains in place; our apparatus of mental concepts continues to be autonomous.

These views are by no means shared by all analytic philosophers; Kripke was mentioned above as an exception. Hardly any attention is paid to them by philosophers of other schools. It may nevertheless be said that neurological science has made more of a general impact on philosophers of the analytic school than on the public in the Western countries at large, particularly in the United States. This exemplifies the scientistic turn that analytic philosophy has recently taken. Scientism is not merely the disposition to regard science as the supreme, perhaps even the only, source of knowledge: it is the tendency to aim at being, toward science, *plus catholique que le Pape*. The scientistically inclined treat the science of their day as final truth, ignoring contention between rival theories and the equally frequent displacement of a reigning theory by one recognized as superior. They project the successes of current science into an imaginary future, and argue from the future triumphs that they hypothesize as if they were certain to be achieved. They employ scientific concepts in preference to others that have served us well and have not been shown to be misbegotten, as if truth were to be located only in a conceptual system devised for a particular theoretical purpose. As scientists themselves often do, they attribute to the methods scientists employ, with imperfect agreement among themselves, an exclusive claim to rationality. In short, instead of maintaining a critical eye toward science and its practitioners, as they ought to do toward them and everything else, especially if they are or purport to be philosophers, their attitude is that of worshippers. It is greatly to be deplored that such an attitude has infected a great many philosophers of the analytic school, because it will be an obstacle to their reconciliation with philosophers of other schools. Neurological science has nevertheless made more of an impact on philosophers of the analytic school, particularly in the United States, than on the public in Western countries at large. This exemplifies the scientistic turn that analytic philosophy has recently taken. Scientism is the disposition to regard the natural sciences as the only true channel of knowledge. So regarding them implies that the idea that philosophy has a subject matter or a method of its own must be discarded: if it is to contribute to knowledge at all, it must be continuous with the natural sciences, as Quine has always maintained, and its task reduced to that of adding ornamentation to the theories of the scientists.

Natural scientists do not, like mathematicians, aim at using concepts fixed by precise, universally accepted definitions; they are satisfied that the content be determined by the concepts' role within their theories and connection, when it is direct, with observation. Natural science produces theories that can be transmitted from one scientist to another; such theories may be disputed and revised, but at no stage do they depend on presentation by their originators. Natural scientists are not concerned, as philosophers are, to scrutinize the concepts with which human beings operate. Philosophy produces explorations, which may indeed generate theories; but great philosophical writing never yields all that it contains on a single reading or to a single reader. It aims not to formulate theses detachable from their authors' expression of them, but to provide insight into very complex conceptual tangles; that is why we cannot compose a résumé of all that Plato or Kant had to say and encapsulate it in textbooks, removing the need to go on reading their works. The concepts explored by philosophers are those in terms of which we think and engage with one another: to describe them is to delineate their roles within what Wittgenstein called our "form of life." The concepts that figure in scientific theories are, by contrast, ones that have as little as possible to do with our form of life: they are fashioned to depend as little as possible for their explanation on human modes of perception or the position of humanity in the cosmos. Much of philosophy—ethics and the philosophy of the mind, for example—is directly concerned with what is distinctively human. Much, such as the metaphysics of space and time, is not: its focus of interest is reality as it is independently of us. But all philosophical inquiry must start with *our* concepts—scientific as well as everyday. Philosophy aims to explore the structure of human thought and by doing so to clarify our conceptions of reality. The scientistically inclined spurn philosophical reflection so conceived; they prefer to employ scientific concepts, as if truth were to be located only in conceptual systems developed for specialized theoretical purposes. They replace philosophical explanations with "naturalized" versions. Such "naturalized" theories may explain notions to do with meaning in terms that wholly prescind from human use of language in communication; they therefore deny that a theory of meaning need yield an account of a speaker's understanding of linguistic utterances. Or they may explain our having the concepts that we do in terms of their supposed evolutionary advantages. This is not philosophy; but it is not science either. It is the result of the bedazzlement of those who have undertaken one manner of intellectual inquiry by the successes of another. That so many philosophers of the analytic school have suffered this bedazzlement will be an obstacle to a reconciliation between that school and its rivals.

This is not at all to say that psychology is irrelevant to philosophy. Psychology as a science was born in philosophy departments, and remains a discipline with much to teach its mother and much to learn from her. We are conscious beings, and our actions are governed by our conscious wills and our conscious decisions. But our observations and the knowledge we derive from them depend on much that takes place within us at a level below consciousness, as do our consciously performed actions. A simple example noted by Gareth Evans is the direction of sound. When we hear a sound, we usually hear it as coming from some particular direction. At the conscious level, this is primitive: we do not derive our sense of the direction from which the sound is coming from something else that we observe through our ears or any other organ. The direction of the sound is simply presented as one of its features. In fact, our apprehension of the sound's direction is derived from a feature of our auditory sensation that we do not consciously notice, namely the minute difference between the time at which the sound enters one ear and that at which it enters the other. This feature is processed to determine the direction of the sound and deliver it to our consciousness, at a level below consciousness. We do not observe the difference between the times at which the sound strikes the two ears and work out from that where it is coming from: our brains do so.

It is the same with action. You pick up a pair of scissors in order to snip off a thread from your clothing. The intentional action is a conscious one; conscious also is the motive for which you do it. But the precise direction in which your hand moves, and the movements of your fingers in grasping the scissors, you are not capable of describing; they are controlled by processing in your brain that occurs at a subpersonal level. The acquisition of a skill by instruction and practice involves driving down into the sub-personal level what in the beginning is highly conscious. When you first try to punt, for example, you have no idea how to control the direction of the boat, which will probably go in a circle. You are then shown the angle at which to throw down the punt pole in order to send the boat in this direction or that, and how to correct any error. You practice, bearing these instructions in mind. After sufficient practice, the proper use of the punt pole becomes "second nature." Now you may think, "I must avoid that oncoming canoe," and steer skillfully to keep out of its way, without the least conscious thought of the movements of the pole by which you accomplish this. You can still bring them to mind if you have to instruct a beginner; but when you are simply punting for pleasure, the technique has been buried in a level below consciousness.

The problem presents itself how to explain the relation between conscious thought and action and the subpersonal operation of our brains; this is a modern version of the ancient problem of how mind and body interact. Such problems are the proper concern of the philosopher as well as the psychologist. For many psychologists, the solution has to be that everything that lies at the conscious level—the identification of the object to be acted on, the action upon it, the motive for which the action was performed—has a correlated operation in the brain, even though the physiologists have not yet discovered it. For such psychologists, consciousness therefore becomes an epiphenomenon, without any genuine causal role. The problem then arises why consciousness should exist at all. The problem is obviously spurious and the view of consciousness as an epiphenomenon absurd, but the problem remains how conscious perception and thought, conscious intentional activity, and the brain processing that takes place at a level inaccessible to consciousness are involved with one another. Plainly the solution will depend heavily upon the discoveries of the physiologists and the experimental psychologists. But equally it is one to which philosophical reflection must make an essential contribution.

6

RELIGION AND PHILOSOPHY

Although conflicts can occur, science is not intrinsically a rival to philosophy. Is religion?

Among one circle of opinion, it has become fashionable to deny that religious faith requires us to subscribe to any propositions; the word "proposition" is usually pronounced by those who hold this view in a sneering tone. Propositions are not in themselves to be sneered at: they form the contents of our beliefs, as, for example, that some injured person will die if he is not taken at once to the hospital. The thesis is, therefore, the paradoxical one that faith does not require any beliefs. It will be replied that what faith demands is not belief *that* one or another state of affairs obtains, but belief *in* whatever the particular religion holds out as the proper object of devotion. Such a distinction between belief-that and belief-in has very little substance. You believe in ghosts if you believe that there are such things as ghosts; someone who declares that he does not believe in medical doctors means to say that he does not believe that they can do much to cure or prevent disease. To believe in a person in the sense of trusting that person, you must believe first that that person exists, and second that that person can be relied on to act in certain ways. The supposed distinction is spurious. Although it may be true that no principle is not believed by some Hindu, it is preposterous to deny that an adherence to any other religion than Hinduism requires consent to certain propositions: for Judaism, Christianity, and Islam, consent in the first place to the proposition that God exists.

In a similar spirit, it is contended by some that, although there may be articles of faith to which consent is required by those who profess a given religion, the doctrines they articulate do not state facts. This contention is equally absurd. Some philosophers regard *facts*—that the planets go in elliptical orbits about the sun, for example—as among the components of reality; complexes, in a different category from the objects that are their constituents, but in the same sense parts of the external world. To be true, on this account, a proposition must correspond to, that is, must match one of these facts. There are fatal objections to this view. No reasonable explanation can be given of the required relation of correspondence. If the truth of any proposition consists in correspondence to a fact, the individuation and structure of facts must tally exactly with the individuation and structure of true propositions: there must be negative as well as affirmative or positive facts, general facts as well as particular ones, conditional facts in addition to categorical ones. The implausibility of peopling reality with such a variety of complex entities provides a strong reason for adopting the alternative view, with which I myself would concur, that facts are simply to be identified with true propositions: they together characterize reality, but they do not compose it; they are *about* reality, but they are not *components* of it. Whichever view be adopted, there must be a precise correlation between facts and true propositions. If a religion requires its adherents to consent to certain propositions, that is, to acknowledge the truth of those propositions, then they must recognize them as stating facts: there are no true propositions that do not state facts.

Those who accept some religion but are disposed to deny that its doctrines state facts are probably using the word "fact" to mean "what can be established by observation." Not even such a deviant use of the word can justify them, if they are Christians, in withholding the status of fact from some Christian doctrines: if Christ rose from the dead, Saint Mary Magdalen and other disciples were able to observe that he had done so. That Christ's mother was conceived without the stain of original sin, by contrast, was not an observable fact: there is no instrument for detecting that stain. If no article of the creed stated an observable fact, there might be some point in distinguishing factual and nonfactual truths by reference to their observability, but many articles do so.

Since the different religions do put forward certain propositions as to be accepted by their adherents, they throw up philosophical problems about the interpretation of those propositions, just as science throws up philosophical problems about the interpretation of its theories. This is especially true of Christianity, which has a particular disposition, celebrated by G. K. Chesteron in his book *Orthodoxy*, to hold apparent incompatibles in tension. For a believer, such a problem is similar to that of the interpretation of quantum mechanics. In both cases he is confronted by a proposition or theory that he takes himself to have good reason to accept as true, but that is very difficult to understand or show to be consistent; only philosophical reflection on it can attain such an understanding or resolve its apparent inner contradictions. A great part of theology is occupied by just such philosophical consideration of religious doctrines. An unbeliever is in a different position. He has no prior reason to consider the doctrines true; they do not have the prestige of science behind them, and cannot claim to have been the foundation of successful predictions. They present philosophical problems that may not concern him greatly, though they may sometimes strike him as being of interest. Insofar as they are claimed to rest on revelation, it is not his business as a philosopher to decide whether, if they are *consistent*, they are true; but it is very much his business to determine whether they are consistent and therefore capable of being true. Since he has no prior reason to suppose them true, he may very well reach the conclusion that they are *not* consistent.

The primary article of faith for the theistic religions is of course that there is a God. This doctrine stands quite otherwise in relation to philosophy than such specifically Christian doctrines as the real presence of Christ in the Eucharist or the two natures, divine and human, possessed by the one person of Christ. Doctrines of this latter kind help the delivery of revelation, not accessible by reason alone; hence, although theologians have the task of explaining their intelligibility by reasoning of a characteristically philosophical kind, the doctrines cannot figure as components of any strictly philosophical system. The existence of God, however, is held by most believers to be a truth attainable by purely rational thought, without appeal to any extraneous source of knowledge. For some, such as proponents of the ontological argument, unaided reason can arrive at it; for others, it can be attained only by invoking contingent facts about the world, such as are evident to universal observation, without the need for specialized knowledge. Any proposition claiming such an epistemological status thereby falls into the province of the philosopher. He needs first to explain what it means to assert that there is a God, and whether such an assertion has an intelligible meaning. If he decides that it is intelligible, it then becomes his proper business to determine whether there are valid reasons for regarding it as true or for regarding it as false. If he concludes that it is true, he then has further questions to answer about what properties can be ascribed to God. Is God omniscient? Is God omnipotent? Can God change, or is he not in time at all? What does it mean to be in time or not to be in time? Is God good?

If so, how is the goodness of God related to the goodness of a human being? All these questions, and many more, lie within the province of one who is both a philosopher and a theist.

The problem of God's existence is not, of course, just one philosophical problem that arises out of religious belief. It is central for any metaphysician—any philosopher who aims at a comprehensive conception of the nature of reality. For that reason, God has played a predominant role in the systems of many philosophers—Descartes, Spinoza, Malebranche, and Berkeley, to cite only a few examples. And the nonexistence of God has played an equally predominant role in the system of other philosophers—most famously, Nietzsche.

The centrality of the existence or nonexistence of God for these philosophers is not, in my view, due to any error of thought. Our progression, from childhood on, through successive layers of distinction of the objective from the subjective forms in us a desire to understand what things are like in themselves, as opposed to how they appear to us. Science is in large part an attempt to answer this highly general question. An early reflection of this effort was Galileo's distinction between primary qualities such as shape, which we perceive as they are in reality, and secondary qualities such as color, which are propensities to produce in us sensations that may not resemble the physical basis of those propensities. The distinction was accepted by Locke and many other philosophers.

But as science progresses, it becomes doubtful whether it is capable of supplying any ultimate answer to the question how things are in themselves, even as regards the purely physical universe. The process of trying to say how things are in themselves requires the progressive abandonment of concepts that derive from, and are explicable only by reference to, our experience as creatures of a certain size and position in the cosmos and endowed with particular sensory and intellectual faculties. The final outcome of the process of stripping every trace of subjectivity from our descriptions of the external world by dispensing with such concepts is the adoption of models with only an abstract mathematical structure. They differ from purely mathematical systems by the efficacy ascribed to them to affect what we can observe, but their abstract character, their lack of concrete content, dissuades us from supposing that, in them, we have arrived at a knowledge of how things are in themselves. That very notion becomes in consequence dubious. No one who believes in God can dismiss it, however: the way things are in themselves must be the way in which God apprehends them. How far we can approximate to a grasp of this is a further, difficult question. But can the notion be explained or defended at all without appeal to God's knowledge of the world, and hence by anyone who denies that God exists? In my opinion, it cannot: the price of denying that God exists is to relinquish the idea that there is such a thing as how reality is in itself. Whether I am right or wrong, the question is crucial if it is possible to give an intelligible account of the nature of reality.

Thus, although there is no intrinsic conflict between religion and philosophy as a discipline of thought, there is plenty of room for conflict between any given religion and the views of some particular philosopher. Such a philosopher may have reached the conclusion that God does not exist or even that it makes no sense to say that God exists; he is thus in opposition to any of the theistic religions. Even if his opinions do not contradict the doctrines of any religion on so fundamental a matter, he may have reached conclusions incompatible with particular tenets by deciding that they are conceptually impossible. Thus he may repudiate the idea of reincarnation, central to the teaching of several of the Eastern religions, as involving a quite mistaken conception of the soul. He may likewise reject the conception that the individual soul can exist, disembodied, between death and the general resurrection, or deny that a body, once disintegrated, can be identified with one that comes into being thousands of years afterward. Or he may argue that particular doctrines such as that of the Trinity or of transubstantiation are not logically coherent. A philosopher who argues that quantum mechanics is not logically coherent has still to explain its success as a scientific theory. One who argues to the same conclusion about one of the dogmas of religion has only to explain away its pretensions as divinely revealed.

Each religion presents its adherents not with a comprehensive conception of reality, but with salient features of such a conception that enable them to do two things: to decide how they should live their lives and to make some sense of what happens by attaching a significance and purpose to it. We nowadays know much more of what happens in the world than our forefathers did, and truly a great deal of it seems very hard for a believer in an omnipotent God who cares about mankind to make any sense of. Nevertheless, religion belief endows our lives with a point, different for different religions, that for an unbeliever it is meaningless even to seek. A religious faith does not embody a metaphysics: there is still much work for the believing metaphysician to do, as indeed for a believer working in any other department of philosophy. But a religious faith has a strong bearing on metaphysics and on other branches of philosophy, so metaphysical and other philosophical conclusions can easily prove incompatible with it. A believer who devotes himself to philosophy must not do so with the intention of devising arguments to defend the tenets of his religion, or he ceases to act as a philosopher rather than an advocate or apologist. As a philosopher, he must follow where the argument leads. If it appears to lead to a conclusion contrary to his religious belief, he must still present it; he may acknowledge that he is convinced that the conclusion cannot be correct, even though he cannot see how to avoid it. Very few philosophical arguments survive unscathed by criticism; it is only by putting them forward to be honed by ensuing discussion that philosophy can progress.

7

RELIGION AND MORALITY

An identification of the way things are in reality with the way they are apprehended by God naturally demands that we attribute knowledge to God. An identification of the principles of morality with the way God wants us to behave similarly demands that we attribute a will to God concerning human actions, though not necessarily one concerning his own actions, which would allow questions such as why God created the world or any of the objects in it. Not all human religions have imposed moral precepts upon their adherents, but all those known as "world religions" have made such a firm connection between their practice and the practice of the moral virtues. Living a morally upright life is, in the teaching of any of these religions, essential for salvation, however the particular religion conceives of it. A tight connection between religion and morality may be held to distinguish the advanced religions from more primitive ones such as the religion of classical Greece, greatly to the credit of the advanced religions. But these religions do not merely exhort their followers to live virtuous lives; they lay down what they take to be the correct principles of morality.

These may be challenged by philosophers and others; Professor Bernard Williams asserts with satisfaction that no one now regards chastity as a virtue. It is a mistake to believe that there is a universal morality shared among all human beings, or all civilized human beings. There is, no doubt, a consensus about the right way to behave in everyday life, not toward other people in general but toward those regarded as equals; but this covers only a few of our actions. Beyond that, religions differ almost as much in the moral principles they proclaim as in their beliefs about the world and the destiny of men and women. Christian morality is distinctive, and goes back to apostolic times. In sexual matters it is severe, demanding monogamy, unlike Hinduism, Islam, and the Old Testament patriarchs, and rejecting divorce, unlike Judaism and Islam. It also condemns suicide, in opposition to the ancient Hindu practice of widows' burning themselves on their husbands' funeral pyres, and to the demands made by personal honor in Japan, in ancient Rome, and among British gentlemen; the ethic of honor is opposed by Christian humility and forgiveness. Above all, Christ taught that there is no one who does not count: those of a different race, those of lower caste or none at all, slaves—all are our neighbors.

The Catholic Church claims to teach with divine authority the contents of revelation, but holds that much of the moral law is accessible to all human beings by the use of reason. As there is doctrinal development that draws out what had only been implicit in the original revelation, so there can be moral development leading us to perceive as wrong what we had previously taken to be allowable. This includes slavery and torture; the Church is now moving toward condemning capital punishment, which its moral theologians have traditionally rated as legitimate. The traditional Catholic teaching laying down the conditions for a just war hardly needs reconsideration, since modern weapons of mass destruction render it obsolete by preventing any present or future war from meeting these conditions; and this fact has in effect been recognized by the Church. The confession of past wrongs done by Catholics organized in St. Peter's by Pope John Paul II went far to repudiate many acts that have besmirched the Church's history—the burning of heretics, the encouragement of anti-Semitism, the Crusades. But it was defective in attributing these wrongs to the actions of individual members and not to the Church as an institution. Catholics accept the claim of the Church to have been founded by Christ and to be protected from erroneous teaching by the Holy Spirit. But they cannot deny that it is also a human institution, and acts in the world as do other human institutions. It is necessary for them to distinguish between its actions that are acts of such a human institution and those that flow from its divine founder or come under the protection of the Spirit. That is a delicate line to draw, but it is plainly of the utmost importance to draw it. Many of the actions included in the public confession in St. Peter's were acts not just of errant individuals, but of the Church as an institution. An adequate repentance and self-correction needs to recognize that.

A religious body can thus come to acknowledge something formerly considered morally right as in truth morally wrong. What authority can its leaders claim for their moral teaching? It is wrong to claim, as Frank Mobbs has done, that to treat a moral precept as part of natural law is to base it solely upon fallible human reason; it may be part of revelation even if accessible without it. Traditional Christian morality stems in great part from the teaching of Christ, of the Epistles and of ancient texts like the *Didache*, and is too integrated a system for a Christian to regard it as mere opinion, but precepts not manifestly part of the original integrated system cannot be taught as with divine authority. Though the Church contrived to slide out of its condemnation of usury, it has difficulty discarding a teaching that some type of action is immoral. Paul VI's encyclical *Humanae Vitae* reiterating the prohibition on contraception illustrates this. This encyclical greatly damaged the respect of the faithful for the Catholic Church's moral teaching in general, since many of them do not accept the ban on contraceptives, and in the confessional many priests surreptitiously collude with their rejection of it. But it has also damaged the integrity of Catholic moral theology.

The encyclical did not merely reaffirm a long-standing tradition: it also dealt with something quite new—the Pill. The condemnation of its use for a contraceptive purpose accorded with the manner in which it had been usual to say why it was wrong to use other devices for that purpose, namely precisely because of the purpose. But the Church's recognition that the use by a husband and wife of the "natural" or rhythm method, whereby they confine sexual intercourse to infertile periods, is morally legitimate denied it the right to hold the purpose of reducing the frequency or number of pregnancies to be in itself wrong. A condemnation of the use of contraceptive devices such as condoms could not therefore be consistently based upon their intended purpose, only on a claim that an act involving such a device was intrinsically wrong, regardless of the purpose—for instance, on the ground that it violated the integrity of the marriage act. Such a claim would assimilate such an act to other deviations from normal intercourse condemned by Christian tradition, such as those now generally referred to as oral and anal sex. But, if the prohibition of contraceptives were based on such a ground, the Pill really did pose a new question, since its use could not be described as violating the integrity of the marriage act. Instead, the encyclical condemned its use when the purpose was contraceptive, that is, to reduce the frequency or number of pregnancies, and for that purpose alone. Moral philosophy cannot accommodate such a prohibition.

A certain type of act, defined by a given form of description, may be intrinsically wrong. If so, it can never be morally justified by an ulterior purpose, however commendable; this is what is meant by saying that the end does not justify the means. For instance, to give someone a fatal dose of poison must in all circumstances be wrong: even if the purpose is to frustrate the known plan of the victim to massacre an entire family, it will still be wrong. It would be a misuse of the principle of double effect to appeal to it in justification of such a murder. The poisoner could not legitimately argue, "What I was doing was to save that family from slaughter; I had no interest in the death of my victim in itself." Nor can the dropping of the atomic bomb on Nagasaki be justified on the score that what was being done was to end the war and the deaths of the inhabitants were side effects. Double effect can be invoked only when the act is in itself morally legitimate, even though in the particular circumstances it will have foreseeable evil side effects. Nothing can be a side effect if it is the means by which the objective of the act is realized. The poisoner cannot claim the death of his victim as a side effect: it is only through the death of the victim that he saves the family from massacre. Conversely, an act that is not intrinsically morally illegitimate may be wicked if it is done for an evil purpose. Thus to give someone a piece of information that it is not in itself wrong to impart in order to humiliate him or to prompt him to do something shameful is rendered an immoral act by the intention with which it was done.

The use of the Pill by a married woman with contraceptive intent does not fall into either of these categories. No one supposes that it is intrinsically wrong for a woman to take the Pill, for example for its original purpose of regularizing irregular periods. It has been persuasively argued that the Pill may be legitimately taken with contraceptive intent, for instance by a nun who knows herself in danger of rape. Equally, the intention, on the part of a married couple, of reducing the frequency or number of the wife's pregnancies is, as already noted, recognized by the Church as legitimate and, in appropriate circumstances, praiseworthy. In the ruling of *Humanae Vitae*, we have therefore a condemnation as morally wrong of an act not intrinsically wrong but held to become wrong when it is done for a particular end, even though that end is likewise not in itself wrong. It is incomprehensible how this could be so; it is impossible to think of a parallel—at least, I have not been able to think of one. Whatever may be thought about the maintenance in the encyclical of the traditional teaching on other methods of contraception, the prohibition on the use of the Pill is indefensible on the basis of moral theology as it has always been previously understood, and throws the moral teaching of the Church into confusion.

Pope Paul VI did many good things, yet his most important action, the issuing of *Humanae Vitae*, has engendered unresolved moral chaos. This chaos is most sharply seen in the confusion about condoms in countries where AIDS has tragically become pandemic. Some Church authorities oppose the use of condoms in an absolute and doctrinaire spirit: they proclaim that the only allowable course for a married couple who know one of them to be HIV-positive, or do not know that both are not, is complete sexual abstinence. No doubt, if to use a condom is in all circumstances morally wrong, that is correct advice. But it is irresponsible to give it without adding emphatically that to risk infecting one's marriage partner—or, indeed, anyone else—with a terrible and fatal disease is immeasurably more wicked than to use a condom or consent to its use. Some Church authorities with a more balanced sense of moral priorities have sought to justify the use of condoms by appeal to the principle of double effect. If the use of a condom is wrong only when it is done to prevent conception, like the use of the Pill according to Paul VI, then no justification is needed when it is done for a different purpose, such as to protect against infection. If, on the other hand, the use of a condom is intrinsically wrong, as violating the integrity of the marriage act, it follows from what was said above about double effect that to try to justify it by appeal to that principle is an abuse of the principle. But the existence of the horrifying disease of AIDS should surely prompt some rethinking about the blanket condemnation of contraceptives, including condoms. Perhaps it was a mistake to class all use of them as intrinsically wrong. There are actions that ought not to be performed in ordinary circumstances but are not wrong in exceptional cases. An assertion not actually false as stated but bound to mislead is an example. Might it not be right to classify the use of contraceptives, other than those that produce abortions, under this head? May not large external circumstances provide a genuine clue to the will of God?

Religion forces our attention upon our successes and failures in the effort to act rightly, and gives a resonance to that effort that the mere goal of uprightness cannot have. It imparts to the exercises of prayer and meditation an intensity lacked by most other doings of everyday life. In particular, it endows certain events, lying in the distant past, with a special significance and, by its ritual and accompanying religious exercises, enables them at successive yearly times to become present to the devotee rather than merely important happenings remote in the past; they become for him as if he were there when they took place.

Why should the unbeliever, for whom all this is illusion, for whom nothing actually happens but the performance of the ritual, feel a hostility toward any of this, rather than a sympathy allied to regret that he cannot participate? Rejecting religion often animates the unbeliever with a hatred of it as passionate as the believer's devotion to it. Disbelief is not itself a kind of religion, because it lacks all religion's other attributes; but it is often imbued with a similar intensity of feeling. Some of this has a political motive, as with the opposition of the Left to the Church in Italy and France; one could almost speak of this as tribal, like the hostility of Orthodox to Catholics in Greece, based on the memory of the capture of Constantinople in the Fourth Crusade. But insofar as it has a rational basis, it is those crimes committed by religious believers, in the name of their religion, against people of a different creed.

A large part of what prompted those crimes stemmed from the prevalent conception of faith. Faith did not, on this conception, command the believer merely to trust his beliefs or to hang on to them: it commanded him to invest them with certainty. He must not allow a suspicion that they were not true ever to so much as cross his mind. If someone is literally certain that his faith is the uniquely true one, it is likely to appear to him that he is justified in doing everything he can to prevent the dissemination of divergent opinions and to enforce acceptance of his own. Error, he will think, has no rights; hence the persecutions and cruelties that have brought about many Christian martyrdoms and at the same time have disfigured the various branches of Christianity in the past. In our times a widespread change of attitude has come over some Christians in this regard. They have come to understand how intimately anyone's religious faith serves to determine his identity, whether that faith is, in their own eyes, mistaken or sound. They have learned how precious to each person his own faith is, and how deeply wounding to him is any manifestation of contempt for it or any insult directed to it. They have realized how unjust it is to compel anyone to abandon his religion or to adopt another, and how intolerable an invasion that is of the inner citadel of his being. Where it was in times past the practice of the churches to trample on religious freedom, freedom for all religions has become a principle sincerely proclaimed by them.

This change of heart has not as yet received any adequate theological foundation. The Second Vatican Council gave a new assessment of the status of separated Christian churches, and also of the Jewish faith; but there is obviously an equal need for a reassessment of the status of non-Christian religions generally. There is probably also a need for a revised conception of what is demanded by the virtue of faith. Unhappily, no such change of heart is perceptible among those who have no religion, as was evident from their reactions to the Rushdie affair in Britain, and from other manifestations of the hatred of Islam which infests most of Europe. Nor is it perceptible among the followers of the non-Christian religions. Religious intolerance is on the increase in the world at large; for instance; Hindu attacks on Muslim and Christian buildings and people in India, and Muslim attacks on Christians in Egypt, Nigeria, and the Moluccas. Such violence and such injustice are deplorable in themselves; it is also to be deplored that devotees of any religion should so act as to appear to justify the feelings of those who hate religion as much.

8

THE INFLUENCE OF GOTTLOB FREGE

Bernard Bolzano (1781–1848) was a great philosopher, and certainly the greatest Czech philosopher—perhaps the only great Czech philosopher. Bolzano was also a great mathematician, as well as a moral and political philosopher and theologian. On a brief visit to Prague, however, I was unable to find a statue or plaque to him, or a street or square named after him. It might be surmised that this was because Bolzano wrote in German, not in Czech; yet Franz Kafka is everywhere celebrated in Prague, and Kafka wrote in German. Possibly Czechs of the present day do not greatly value mathematics or philosophy.

In the Appendix to Chapter 10 of the Prolegomena of 1900 to his *Logische Untersuchungen* (*Logical Investigations*), Edmund Husserl sang a paean of praise to Bolzano, adding some highly disparaging comments on Bolzano's contemporary Hegel. Gottlob Frege was born the year Bolzano died, and died himself in 1925. In both his philosophy of logic and his philosophy of mathematics he was Bolzano's successor; although there is no evidence that Frege ever read Bolzano, they had many philosophical views in common.

Husserl's first book, *Philosophie der Arithmetik* (*Philosophy of Arithmetic*) (1891), had been suffused with psychologism, the strategy of explaining concepts by reference to the inner mental operations by which it was supposed that they were acquired. In 1894 Frege published a vitriolic, and not completely fair, review of the book; this was his most sustained critique of psychologism, to which he was implacably opposed throughout his career. Husserl may have been wounded by Frege's review, but by the time he came to write his Prolegomena, he had come around to the same view, for the Prolegomena consists of a far longer denunciation of psychologism, using many arguments very similar to those used by Frege.

At the turn of the twentieth century German philosophy was awash with a multitude of different currents, among them a rather crude materialism and different varieties of neo-Kantianism. But in 1901 anyone who had read both Frege's writings and Husserl's *Logische Untersuchungen* would not have seen their philosophical positions as far removed from each other. Yet Husserl went on to be the founder of the phenomenological school, while Frege was the grandfather of analytical philosophy. What made him its progenitor?

Frege was not a professional philosopher but a professional mathematician. At the beginning of his career he conceived the ambition of putting arithmetic on a firm foundation. Arithmetic, here, comprises both number theory—the theory of natural numbers—and analysis—the theory of real and complex numbers. Frege's terminology was inherited from an old-fashioned conception of mathematics as divided into arithmetic—the science of number and quantity—and geometry—the science of space. Frege was deeply interested in geometry, especially projective geometry; but he consistently regarded it as having a quite different epistemological basis from arithmetic. Geometry, for him, though a priori, rested on intuition; but he was at one with

Bolzano in believing that to establish the truths of arithmetic, no appeal to intuition was needed. Frege understood a foundation for arithmetic to involve an analysis of its concepts, including the concepts of natural number and of real number; an isolation of its fundamental laws; and a convincing account of our justification for believing those laws. To the large project of constructing an incontrovertibly correct foundation for arithmetic he dedicated his entire career.

Frege believed that the first step in carrying out this project must be the construction of a logic adequate for mathematical reasoning. The long history of logic since Aristotle had not succeeded in attaining the ability to represent the modes of inference employed in the proof of even the simplest mathematical theorems. But Frege did not aim merely at representing such inferences; he wanted to construct a language in which they could be carried out by means of formal rules. The need for such a language lay in the necessity, if arithmetic was to be shown independent of intuition, of avoiding two opposite mistakes. If mathematical reasoning were solely to be conducted informally, its transitions judged correct only by the subjective impression of their correctness, it would be possible that a tacit reliance on intuition would be overlooked and an inference accepted as purely logical when in fact it rested on the basis of some compelling appeal to intuition. But the opposite mistake would also be possible: an inference might be so expressed as to make it appear to rest on intuition, when in fact it could be accomplished by logical means uncontaminated by appeal to anything extraneous. To establish the fundamental basis of arithmetic and, in particular, its independence from intuition would require deriving its basic principles by formalized proofs in a language whose rules of inference were purely logical and strictly formal.

In order to present a language in which this could be done, governed by just such rules of inference, Frege published his first book, the *Begriffsschrift* of 1879. This astonishing short work constituted the invention of modern mathematical logic: in it, Frege gave, in a notation that no one has imitated, complete formalizations of classical sentential logic and first-order predicate logic, and an important foray into second-order logic, involving quantification over properties and relations. The work was thus a revolutionary contribution to formal logic, enabling it, for the first time in many centuries, to handle the kind of reasoning customary in mathematical proofs and showing how to fashion a language in which such proofs could be carried out in accordance with logic's formal rules of inference. But it would misrepresent Frege's ideas to regard the book simply as contributing to formal logic. It contained only small sections in prose, devoted to the underlying principles of analysis governing the formal system, but to Frege these were integral to the whole. He drew no distinction between formal and philosophical logic; the two formed for him a single science.

Partly for this reason, he was led to make great incursions into the realms proper to philosophy; also, his project demanded an analysis of the fundamental concepts of arithmetic and an account of the basis of our knowledge of its laws, in his sense of the term "arithmetic." He came to believe that arithmetic, in this sense, had no axioms peculiar to it: its concepts were definable in purely logical terms and its fundamental laws were derivable from pure logic. In 1884 he published a brilliant little book, *Die Grundlagen der Arithmetik* (*The Foundations of Arithmetic*), in which he expounded this view, demolished alternative theories, and gave a preliminary sketch of the logical derivation of the fundamental laws of number theory. He devoted the years from 1886 to 1890, during which he published nothing, to a thorough revision of his logic, formal and philosophical. The most important change in his formal system was the addition of an operator for forming terms for classes (more exactly, for value ranges standing to functions as classes stand to properties or, in Frege's terminology, to concepts). The most important change in his ideas about the meanings of words and symbols was the introduction of the famous distinction between *Sinn* and *Bedeutung*. It is difficult to find a translation for these two terms faithful to Frege's intentions in using them: the best, though still very imperfect, choice in English is to use "sense" and "reference" respectively.

In 1893 Frege published the first volume of his monumental *Grundgesetze der Arithmetic* (*Basic Laws of Arithmetic*), which was to carry out his project of providing a definitive foundation for arithmetic in full detail. The book was filled with rigorous formal proofs in Frege's eccentric and difficult notation. In 1902, just as the second volume was due to appear, Frege received a letter from Bertrand Russell, informing him of the contradiction that Russell had discovered in his formal theory. It was derivable from Frege's axiom governing classes or value ranges: it was the celebrated contradiction of the class of classes that are not members of themselves. Frege hastily devised a weakening of his axiom that he hoped would avoid the contradiction and added it as an appendix to volume II of his work, which came out in 1903; in it he began but did not conclude an exposition of his theory of real numbers. Frege's weakened axiom for classes blocked Russell's contradiction but was not in fact consistent; only a cursory check was not enough to show that, whether or not it were consistent, it did not allow the formal proofs that had filled volume I to go through. It took Frege until mid-1906 to convince himself that he was unable to remedy the fault in his system. At that point he faced the realization that his life's work, to construct a sound foundation for arithmetic, had irreparably failed.

He sat down and wrote a small fragment to answer the question what survived from the work on which he had spent his whole career; this fragment has survived among those transcripts of his papers that did not perish with the originals during the bombing of Münster during the Second World War. The part of his work that had survived was the logic, apart from the theory of classes: the formal and the philosophical logic, which, for him, were one. Well before Frege's death in 1925, his work was largely forgotten, with the principal exceptions of Russell and of Wittgenstein, who revered him. But from the 1970s onward there has been among analytic philosophers a great reawakening of interest in his writing. In all universities in which analytic philosophy is taught, he is now recognized not merely as the founder of mathematical logic but as a thinker of profound importance who was the grandfather of analytic philosophy; all philosophy students at such universities are required to study him. In the last few years there has been a strong revival of interest in Frege's philosophy of arithmetic, but what has been influential has been precisely that part of his work which, in 1906, he felt to be unscathed from the disaster wrought by Russell's discovery of the contradiction. His contribution to formal logic had long been absorbed into the general body of mathematical logic, but the philosophical underpinning he gave it continues to be regarded by analytical philosophers as of fundamental value to philosophical logic and philosophy of language. When, in 1906, Frege listed items of his work that had survived the disaster, he picked them from the system as he had revised it in the silent interval before 1891—his mature doctrine, not that which had underlain the *Begriffsschrift* and the *Grundlagen*; and it has been his mature thought that has become so influential and so highly regarded since the 1970s.

Much of Frege's writing is unquestionably philosophical rather than mathematical in character, but he trespassed very little over the boundaries of two restricted philosophical areas—logic and the philosophy of mathematics. How does it come about that one who was not a philosopher by profession and who confined his philosophical writing to so restricted a part of the subject could be perceived as a revolutionary innovator? The reason is this: Frege devised the first systematic theory of meaning, which could also be seen as the first systematic analysis of thought. It does not matter that he did not tackle problems in other parts of philosophy: these are fundamental achievements that, insofar as they are correct, must underlie the rest of philosophy.

9

FREGE'S ANALYSIS OF SENTENCES

What were the leading ideas that made Frege the first proponent of a plausible theory of meaning?

THE CONTEXT PRINCIPLE

The governing principle of Frege's philosophical logic, highlighted in his *Grundlagen*, was that "only in the context of a sentence do the words mean anything." At first sight this so-called context principle contradicts the obvious fact that we understand sentences by understanding the words compounding them; this, as Frege himself insisted, is how we can understand sentences that have never before occurred to us. But to say that it is only in the context of a sentence that a word has meaning is to say that its meaning consists in the contribution that it makes to determining the sense of any sentence containing it: it cannot be understood otherwise. Ideally, such a contribution ought to be uniform from sentence to sentence; that is how we are able to understand new sentences. Natural languages are not ideal, and their words are frequently capable of making different contributions according to the sentences in which they figure and their places therein. But to understand the language properly, we have to know all the different types of contribution each word can make, and how to judge which one it is making to any given sentence; sometimes there is inescapable ambiguity, and no way to judge.

In chapter 49 of his *Philosophische Untersuchungen* (*Philosophical Investigations*), posthumously published in 1953, Ludwig Wittgenstein illustrated Frege's context principle for proper names in the following way (his names are of differently colored squares):

> we might say . . . that a sign "R" or "B," etc., may sometimes be a word and sometimes a sentence. But whether it is a word or a sentence depends on the situation in which it is uttered or written. For instance, if A has to describe complexes of colored squares to B and he uses the word "R" *alone*, we shall be able to say that the word is a description— a sentence. But if he is memorizing the words and their meanings, or if he is teaching someone else the use of the words . . . , we shall not say that they are here sentences. In this situation the word "R," e.g., is not a description: it *names* an element. . . . Naming and describing do not stand on the same level: naming is a preparation for description. Naming is not so far a move in the language game—any more than putting a piece in its place on the board is a move in chess. We may say: *nothing* has so far been done, when a thing has been named. It has not even *got* a name except in the language game.

By "making a move in the language game" Wittgenstein means saying something—making an assertion, asking a question, telling someone what to do, voicing a wish, or the like. When you give some object a name you are not saying anything, only setting up one condition for saying something—just as when, in telling someone the rules of a card game, you say, "The cards rank in this order," you have not stated a rule until you lay down what happens when cards of different ranks are played. Likewise, when you utter a name that has previously been given to some object, you have not yet said anything, unless the name has been uttered in a situation in which, by itself, it is understood as equivalent to a whole sentence, such as "Here comes X." Naming an object, or using some other means of referring to it, has meaning only as an ingredient in the act of saying something about it; and when an object is given a name, the action is significant only because the name is understood as a name, that is, as capable of serving as such an ingredient.

INCOMPLETE EXPRESSIONS

Frege's second most fundamental idea has a somewhat technical explanation of the point underlying it, but was nevertheless essential to his ontology. It was the idea of incomplete expressions. He eschewed the term "predicate," as too bound up with traditional logic, but the bond is now broken, so that we may use it here in preference to Frege's "concept-word." A predicate, according to Frege, is not to be thought of as built up from its component words; rather, it is extracted from some complete sentence by omitting one or more occurrences of some proper name or other singular term. Thus the two sentences "Prince Charles is younger than Prince Charles's mother" and "Queen Elizabeth is younger than Queen Elizabeth's mother" have something in common (other than their obviousness). What they have in common is not just a sequence of words but a feature, to which it is essential that the name serving as grammatical subject also appears in the genitive before "mother." They have a predicate in common, in the sense just explained. The predicate can be represented as "N is younger than N's mother," where the letter "N" indicates the two occurrences of one and the same proper name in either sentence, but together form a gap within the predicate, which constitutes its *argument place*. This predicate is an incomplete expression: the gap or argument place is integral to it; it will become a sentence when the gap is filled by any proper name or singular term. That is why Frege's alternative description of the process of extracting the predicate from a sentence is equivalent: it consists of envisaging the replacement in the sentence of the proper name, in its selected occurrences, by one or another name. An incomplete expression is not, in general, a connected part of a sentence: it is a feature common to different sentences that cannot be displayed, only represented.

In a similar manner, a relational expression (in modern jargon, a two-place predicate) may be formed by removing from a sentence one or more occurrences of each of two proper names; and a functional expression may likewise be formed by removing from some complex singular term one or more occurrences of some proper name. These operations effect the formation of new concepts. Thus by removing all three occurrences of the numeral "7" from the sentence "7 is greater than 1 and the only numbers dividing 7 are 7 and 1" we obtain an expression for the concept of a *prime* number. In the semantic analysis of sentences, the notions of relational and functional expressions are necessary to explain quantification over relations and functions. (They are also necessary for explaining the use of schematic letters for such expressions in logical formulas, but for Frege, what look like schematic letters are to be understood as bound by tacit initial universal quantifiers.)

THE QUANTIFIER-VARIABLE NOTATION

However, (one-place) predicates have a more fundamental use. A sentence may be formed from a predicate by a different means from inserting a term in its argument place, namely by attaching a quantifier to it. Thus by attaching the universal quantifier to the predicate "N is younger than N's mother" we obtain the sentence "For every x, x is younger than x's mother." The notational device of quantifiers and variables bound by them, in place of the insertion of an expression of generality in the argument place of the predicate, was Frege's prime invention that enabled him to compose the first work of the new mathematical logic. It obviated the need for the traditional logic to manhandle every predicate into the form of a grammatical predicate beginning with the copula "is" and dispensing with any repetition of a singular term to which it was attached—a process governed by no formal rules, only the intelligence of the logician. Further, it made redundant the use of compound phrases such as "every dog": a sentence such as "Every dog eats meat" could be represented as "Everything, if it is a dog, eats meat" and "Some dogs bite" as "Something is a dog and bites." ("Every" and "some" can be handled in this way; "most" cannot.) Far more importantly than either of these, it allowed Frege to solve the problem of multiple generality, as in the sentence "Every dog is owned by someone." Here, one word, "someone," that expresses generality stands in the scope of another, "every." The scholastic logicians had wrestled in vain with the problem how to handle such sentences; the quantifier/variable notation solved it at a stroke.

How so? The key is the conception of complex sentences as formed step by step from the simplest (atomic) sentences; this is one exemplification of the principle of compositionality, that the meaning of a sentence can be derived from the meanings of its constituents. In virtue of Frege's account of the formation of predicates from complete sentences, we need no parallel account of the formation of complex predicates from simple ones. A logical connective such as "or" may be explained by laying down that "A or B" is true just in case either "A" or "B" is true. This gives the condition for the truth of a sentence in which "or" is the principal operator. But "or" also occurs in sentences such as "My spectacles are broken, and I shall speak extempore or shall not speak at all," in which it is not the principal operator. It may therefore seem that our explanation of "or" was defective, but that is not so. We need to think of the sentence as formed in two steps from simpler sentences. First, the two sentences, "I shall speak extempore" and "I shall not speak at all" are joined by the connective "or"; in the resulting sentence, "or" is the principal operator, so we know that it is true just in case one of the simpler sentences is true. The second step is to join this sentence to the sentence "My spectacles are broken" by means of the connective "and": we know the condition for the truth of *this* sentence because we know the condition for the truth of its second conjunct, formed at the first step. An explanation of the meaning of a sentence of which a given logical operator is the principal operator thus suffices to explain sentences in which that operator plays a subordinate role.

This is why the quantifier/variable device enabled Frege to express generality occurring in a subordinate position. He explained the universal quantifier only as serving as the principal operator: "For every x, A(x)" will be true just in case the predicate "A(N)" is true of every object; it will be true of a given object if, where "a" names that object, the sentence "A(a)" is true. Let us add the existential quantifier, explained similarly, to Frege's stock of logical operators. (He himself expressed it only by means of negation and the universal quantifier.) Then the sentence "Every dog has an owner" may be built up in the following stages.

1. From "Gertrude owns Fido" we form the predicate "M owns Fido."
2. We attach the existential quantifier to this predicate to obtain the sentence "For some y, y owns Fido."
3. We use "if . . . then" to form from this sentence and "Fido is a dog" the sentence "If Fido is a dog, then for some y, y owns Fido."

4. From this we form the predicate "If N is a dog, then for some y, y owns N."

5. Finally, we attach the universal quantifier to this predicate, to obtain "For every x, if x is a dog, then for some y, y owns x."

The truth of this sentence does not depend on the truth of some sentence of the form "For every x, if x is a dog, then Gertrude owns x." But the sentence into which the existential quantifier was first introduced in the process of construction, namely "For some y, y owns Fido," is to be explained in this way; and that suffices to explain the role of "for some y" in the final sentence.

A frivolous objection to Frege's conception of incomplete expressions is that natural language is averse to multiple occurrences of the same name or singular term within any one sentence: we do not naturally say, "Prince Charles is younger than Prince Charles's mother," but "Prince Charles is younger than his mother." An understanding of personal pronouns requires us to take the shorter sentence as an equivalent of the longer one; in cases of ambiguity or misunderstanding, we have recourse to the more explicit form, as in the absurd dialogue:

A: Prince Charles is younger than his mother.
B: So is Queen Elizabeth.
A: No she isn't: she is his mother.
B: I meant that Queen Elizabeth is younger than Queen Elizabeth's mother, not than Prince Charles's mother.

The use of a pronoun rather than a name in such contexts is unnecessary for conveying what we mean, and sometimes confusing. We do not use pronouns in mathematical formulas: we write:

3 < 2 cubed

Not

$$3 < 2^{it}.$$

It is common to read, in expositions of modern model theory, dismissals of Frege's "bizarre" notion of incomplete entities. Such model theorists interpret one-place predicate letters as sets of elements rather than as concepts, in Frege's sense, under which they fall. This is to emphasize the extensional character of the semantic value of the predicate—for the semantic value of another predicate to be different, there must be at least one element that satisfies one predicate but not the other. Frege's notion of a concept was no different in this regard, however: it is only the word that is misleading. But Frege held that we could come by the notion of a set or class only via that of a concept: a class can be given only as the extension of a concept—the class of objects falling under it—and can only be so understood.

A rejection of Fregean incomplete entities goes with a rejection of Fregean incomplete expressions. This is motivated by a preference for the technique of Alfred Tarski in the semantics of formal languages. In this, formulas are built up not only from atomic *sentences* but also from *open* atomic formulas. An open formula may contain, besides individual constants representing proper names, a number of *free variables*; different atomic formulas forming the basis of some one complex formula may of course contain different free variables. Free variables are a very convenient device, eventually to be assigned elements of the domain. But they are no more than a device: they function as proper names with varying denotations. A proper name with a varying denotation is a chimera; free variables have no genuine linguistic role to play. Frege's analysis of the formation of predicates and other incomplete expressions from complete sentences or terms constitutes a genuine insight into our construction of complex sentences and the formation of complex thoughts, as well as into the formation of concepts in the usual (non-Fregean) sense of the word "concept."

There is, however, a genuine difficulty about Frege's notion. The idea that predicates are extracted from complete sentences, and concepts from complete thoughts, suggests that complete sentences are what we start from. If so, how do we come to grasp their senses, that is, the complete thoughts that they express? We grasp the sense of a complex sentence by understanding how it was built up from atomic sentences, but how do we come to grasp the sense of an atomic sentence? This was a problem to which Frege failed to give adequate attention.

An atomic sentence in a language that conforms with the structure of the formulas in Frege's logical symbolism will be composed of either a proper name or another singular term in the argument place of a (one-place) predicate, e.g., "The Danube is blue," or of two names or terms in the argument places of a relational expression, e.g., "Everest is higher than Nanda Devi." Frege does not describe simple predicates and relational expressions like "N is blue" and "N is higher than M" in different terms from complex ones; they too are incomplete expressions with one or two argument places respectively. This makes it seem as though, according to him, we first conceive of the predicate "N is blue" by imagining the name "the Danube" in the sentence "The Danube is blue" as replaced by some other name such as "the Rhône" or "the Volga." But to understand a predicate so extracted, we must first understand the sentence from which it was extracted. How, then, could we have arrived at an understanding of *it*? This is our problem.

It must be acknowledged that the simple predicate "is blue" is an incomplete expression, carrying an argument place with it, if we are to explain the unity of the sentence "The Danube is blue"—how the name fits together with the predicate to form an expression that *says* something. Furthermore, Frege's explanation of its incompleteness tallies with what the late Gareth Evans called "the generality constraint": we could not understand that sentence unless we knew that other things, e.g., the Rhône, could (truly or falsely) be said to be blue, and indeed, that other things could be said about the Danube, e.g., that it is brown. A simple-minded account, that we separately learn the meanings of the name and of the predicate, and then proceed to stick them together, is therefore ruled out. Only in the context of a sentence do words mean anything. To learn what a name means involves taking it to be a name, that is, taking it as playing one sort of role in a sentence; and to learn what a predicate means involves taking it to be a predicate, that is, taking it as having an argument place and as playing another sort of role in a sentence. But in any sense in which we become aware of the predicate by extracting it from a sentence, the same holds for the name. In the early stages of our acquisition of language, we learn names and predicates together, as forming sentences: to understand an expression of either kind is to grasp that it can occur in different sentences, and that it can be replaced by other expressions of the same kind. That is why there is no question of our understanding even an atomic sentence as an indivisible semantic unity. But we learn the whole practice—a range of names, a range of predicates, and the practice of combining them in order to say something—together, not piecemeal.

10

FREGE'S THEORY OF MEANING

The ideas expounded in the preceding chapter are all
to be found in Frege's work from before 1890, and
most of them in the *Begriffsschrift*. They remained
intact during his mature period, from 1891 to 1906.
But the ideas of that later period have had the great
influence within analytic philosophy. And first
among these is his distinction between sense and
reference.

Frege's initial explanation of his notion of
Bedeutung always treated of the *Bedeutungen* of
singular terms, including proper names: the *Bedeutung* of a name was its bearer, the *Bedeutung* of a
complex term such as a definite description was the
object to which it was used to refer. That is why the
term "reference" has been used to translate *Bedeutung*. But Frege assumed that *Bedeutung* was to be
ascribed to expressions of all the categories he recognized: not just to singular terms but to predicates,
relational and functional expressions, and sentences
themselves. He did not defend this assumption but
simply took it for granted. This is enough to show
that he was not just tendentiously maintaining that
every expression named something; although he

never gave any general characterization of his notion of *Bedeutung*, the use to which he put it shows clearly that he understood the *Bedeutung* of any expression to be its semantic value. The semantic value of an expression is that by which it contributes to determining the truth or falsity of any sentence in which it occurs. Thus the semantic value of a singular term is the object to which it refers: once you know which object that is, you need know nothing else about the term in order to arrive at the truth value of the sentence. Frege took the *Bedeutung* of a whole sentence to be its truth value. For the *Bedeutung* of a predicate, which you might expect him to call a "property," he used the inappropriate term "concept." By this he did not mean what you grasp when you understand the predicate; a concept, in Frege's writings after 1890, was something extensional, in that one concept was identical with another—or rather, stood to it in a relation analogous to identity—if the same objects fell under each. A Fregean concept differed from a class or set, however, in not being a kind of object. Just as the predicate whose *Bedeutung* is the concept has an argument place and is incomplete, so the concept itself is incomplete. It is integral to the being of a concept that it has an argument place for an object.

We can readily understand what it is for a predicate to be incomplete: it is taken from a sentence as having a gap in it, consisting of one or more empty places where some one singular term is to go. Even if the predicate is a simple one like "is blue," it is easy to see that, in order to understand the expression, we have to take it as one to be completed by a singular term and thereby say something about the object to which the term refers. But what does it mean to say that something extralinguistic that the predicate represents is incomplete? We do not arrive at the concept by detaching an object from the *Bedeutung* of a sentence (which is, on Frege's account, a truth value), and what would it mean to speak of "occurrences" of the object within the truth value? The analogy by which we are to understand the incompleteness of concepts is the incompleteness of mathematical functions. Functions, such as the sine function and the function x^2, play a salient role in mathematics. It would be impossible to understand what a function was without first knowing what numbers were; given numbers, the function can only be conceived of as carrying one number into another—$\pi/2$ into 1 or 3 into 9. A function just is something that takes any number as argument and yields some other number as its value for that argument. This provides an analogy for the conception of something to which it is essential that it can take one or another object as argument. In fact, Frege saw it as more than an analogy. For him, a concept is a special kind of function, namely one that carries any object as argument into a truth value as value. An object is to be said to *fall under* the concept if the concept maps it onto the value *true*, and not to fall under it if if maps it onto the value *false*.

We may hereafter substitute the English word "reference" for the German word *Bedeutung*, as long as we remember that we are talking about semantic value, not about subject matter. In a similar way, the reference of a relational expression is a relation, which is doubly incomplete, and that of a functional expression a unary or binary function, correspondingly incomplete. The reference of a quantifier is a *concept of second level*, which maps concepts, rather than objects, onto truth values. Thus the reference of the universal quantifier is the second-level concept *being true of everything*; this (when restricted to human beings) maps the first-level concept *being younger than one's mother* onto the value *true*. Such an expression as "There are exactly five" has a second-level concept as its reference.

A concept is a special kind of function, but it is not any kind of object. Frege maintained a strict distinction between what can meaningfully be said of an object and what can meaningfully be said of a concept. In a logically correct language, a concept, being incomplete, can be linguistically represented only by an incomplete expression—a predicate. If this principle is observed, it is not merely meaningless but impossible to say of a concept what can be said of an object: what is said of an object is expressed by a predicate, into whose argument place another predicate will not fit. The same distinction is to be made between concepts of first and second level. Existence is a concept of second level: the ontological argument for the existence of God is misbegotten because it treats it as a concept of first level.

Notoriously, this doctrine led Frege into paradox: not a grave paradox like Russell's contradiction, but, in my view, a trivial one. The words "concept," "function," and "relation" look like common nouns such as "city" and "river," and hence as though they form first-level predicates when the copula is added. In that case concepts, functions, and relations would be special kinds of objects, as cities and rivers are; when we spoke of the concept woman or the concept prime number, we should be referring to particular such objects. This is obviously contrary to Frege's demarcation of logical types. He rightly made light of it as an awkwardness of language. The solution he tentatively suggested is evidently correct. In natural language, a relative clause can sometimes be used, not to denote an object but predicatively: if I say, "Olivier was what Henry longs to be," the answer to "What is that?" is the predicative phrase "An actor," specifying a concept. Frege suggested that we could use such a clause as "what 'N is blue' refers to" in the same way: to say "The Danube is what 'N is blue' refers to" would be equivalent to saying, "The Danube is blue."

Frege's theory of reference is a semantic theory: it explains, in terms of its composition, how a sentence is determined as true or false. It was in fact the very first systematic semantic theory, and appears explicitly as such in the first volume of Frege's *Grundgesetze*, applied to the symbolic language used in that book. As semantic theory for a natural language, it is obviously defective, since natural language contains many expressions that do not, or do not obviously, fit into Frege's logical categories. But it gave us the first clear idea of what a semantic theory should look like.

The theory of reference was not, however, intended as a theory of meaning. Meaning is the correlate of understanding; hence a theory of meaning for a language must explain what is known by anyone who understands an expression or sentence of that language. But a speaker may know what an expression means without knowing its reference; in particular, he may know what a sentence means without knowing its truth value. A full account of what a speaker knows in knowing the meaning of an expression can never consist in barely stating its reference, not even when the expression is a proper name. To say of someone that he knows, of a certain object, that it satisfies a certain condition—for instance, that of being the bearer of some given name—can be a correct account but never a complete account of the item of knowledge in question. For, as Kant said, every object is given to us in a particular way, and a complete account of such a piece of knowledge must mention the particular way the object is given to the knower. It is the same with concepts and functions. One cannot think of a particular function simply as having a certain value for each possible argument; it must be given by some manner of calculating or defining it. Similarly, one cannot think of a particular concept (in Frege's sense of "concept") simply as having certain objects falling under it; it must be given by some means of establishing that any given object falls under it, or by some condition for an object to do so.

That is why the notion of reference must be supplemented by that of sense. The sense of an expression is the way its reference is given to a speaker. Frege held that with each word of a language is associated a particular way that a speaker or hearer must think of its reference as being given: it is that which constitutes its sense. It is not enough that speaker and hearer should attach the same reference to the word, though for many words of natural language no more can be presumed. Frege often spoke of the conditions that must be satisfied by a scientific language. A scientific language would be one in which deductive reasoning could be carried out with complete assurance; Frege believed that natural languages fell far short of this ideal. It is necessary for a scientific language that two speakers should not merely associate the same reference with any given word but be able to know that this was so. This would be possible only if each word had for both exactly the same sense, so that the reference was given to both in just the same way.

The sense of a complex expression is composed of the senses of its constituent words. It is necessary, for the understanding of any expression, that one knows how it may be put together with other expressions to form a more complex expression or, ultimately, a sentence. Hence one must know of an incomplete expression that it is incomplete, and how its argument place or places must be filled. For that reason the sense of a functional expression is not itself a function; it is incomplete simply in being understood as the sense of a functional expression, one that has a function as its reference. Sense must always be something that can be grasped. In general, the sense of an expression is whatever a speaker of the language must know about it that serves to determine its reference.

A theory of meaning must therefore take the form not of a theory of reference but of a theory of sense; since the sense of an expression is the way its reference is given, a theory of sense for a language must rest on a theory of reference for that language, or at least on the general form of such a theory. Frege took little pains to explain how the senses of expression ought to be specified. One might suppose that the sense of an expression ought merely to be shown by the particular manner in which its reference was laid down, but this would be inadequate. In some instances, the sense of an expression might be given by an actual definition, thus serving to convey the concept it expressed—in an ordinary, non-Fregean sense of "concept"—to one who did not already have it. It would obviously be impossible for this to be done for every word of the language, if the theory of sense is to be noncircular, but it may be demanded that the theory describe in what any speaker's grasp of the sense of the word must consist. In general, we must say that to know the sense of a singular term, he must know the condition for an object to be what it refers to; to know the sense of a predicate, he must know the condition for it to be true of any given object; and so on.

Sense was not for Frege the only component of linguistic meaning. Another component was whatever device is used to indicate the force attached to a sentence. Considered by itself, a sentence simply has a sense—what Frege calls the thought it expresses— and a reference—its truth value. By a "thought" Frege did not mean a mental act of thinking, but the content of such an act—that which may be true or false. The thought expressed by a sentence is determined, according to the composition of the sentence out of its constituent words, by the condition for that sentence to be true. But simply to utter a sentence as expressing some particular thought is not yet to say anything—to make a move in the language game, in Wittgenstein's terminology. In order to make such a move, we have to indicate what we are *doing* in uttering that sentence. If we are asserting that the thought it expresses is true, we must attach assertoric force to the sentence; if we are asking whether the thought is true, we must attach interrogative force—Frege held that a question requiring the answer "Yes" or "No" expresses the same thought as the corresponding declarative sentence. Force can be attached only to a complete sentence. When a sentence is used as a subordinate or coordinate clause in a complex sentence, it expresses the same thought and has the same truth value as when it is uttered on its own, but it has neither assertoric nor interrogative force attached to it.

As well as sense and force, there is also what Frege called "coloring." The coloring of an expression is that part of what it conveys that does not affect the condition for the truth of any sentence in which it occurs. Thus the words "dead" and "deceased" express the same sense, but differ in coloring. Plainly, there are many ways expressions or sentences may differ in meaning, but neither in sense nor in force, and these are important both in ordinary converse and in literature. But Frege himself did not explore these and was not greatly interested in them. Yet, despite some deficiencies in his account, Frege had achieved what no philosopher before him had come near to doing. He had constructed a systematic theory of linguistic meaning, and thereby a systematic theory of the thoughts expressible in language.

Since it is only in the context of a sentence that a word has meaning, the sense of any expression must always be conceived as a contribution to the sense of a sentence in which the expression figures. The content of a sentence—the thought it expresses— is determined by the condition for its truth, so the sense of any expression must always be conceived as contributing to whether what is asserted or asked holds true or not.

Frege's notion of a thought resembles Bolzano's notion of *Satz an sich*—what is called by philosophers writing in English a "proposition"; in referring to Bolzano, we may call it a proposition in itself or a thought, not understood as mental. Frege was particularly insistent that thoughts are not contents of the mind. In saying this, he was contrasting thoughts with sensations and mental images, which he called collectively "ideas" (*Vorstellungen*). They are subjective and private: only I can feel my pain. Thoughts, by contrast, are objective and common to many: to deny this is to deny that one man can disbelieve the very same thing as another believes. Mathematical theorems, scientific laws, and historical truths are thoughts: they can be communicated, and they hold good whether or not they are known or believed.

Frege divided reality into three realms. First is the external world, inhabited by material objects, including our own bodies.

Second is, for each of us, the inner world of his sensation and imagination. And third is the realm within which thoughts and their component senses subsist. As we can perceive the objects of the external world, so we can grasp thoughts objectively existing within the third realm; in fact, it is only through our grasp of thoughts that our inner sensations are converted into perceptions of outer objects.

Frege's theory of the third realm is, plainly, a piece of philosophical mythology; but the extrusion of thoughts from the mind, initiated by Bolzano and so strongly insisted on by Frege, was a step of the first importance: it was the precursor of the linguistic turn. By denying the mental character of thoughts Frege ruled out psychologistic accounts of the sense of linguistic expressions or of concepts in the non-Fregean sense; the right kind of account was that which explained them as going to determine the condition for the truth of a sentence or a thought. Psychologism was for him an enemy because it made thoughts subjective, and severed the connection between them and truth. He located thoughts in a third realm because he wanted to safeguard their objectivity and ability to be grasped by many. If this mythology is repudiated, where are they to be located? It was an inevitable step to take language to be their home. A language is shared by many, as a thought can be grasped by many.

A language, as a social institution, is external to any individual speaker. The meanings of its words are not subjectively associated with them: they are objectively constituted by the common practice of speaking the language. Language has all the properties for which Frege invented the third realm: the extrusion of thoughts from the mind led by a natural progress of reflection to the placing of language in the center of philosophical inquiry.

Was it only by a subsequent conversion of Frege's conception of the third realm that the linguistic turn came about, or was Frege himself in part responsible for it? Were his analyses analyses of sentences or of thoughts? At first sight, we must say, "Of thoughts." To attain a logic capable of handling generality, he did not produce a thoery of how the expressions of generality we use in natural language function; he invented a means of expressing it quite different from those we use in natural language. He did not explain such a sentence as "every dog has an owner" by a theory of the significance of phrases such as "every dog" and (when not preceded by the copula) "an owner," a theory such as the theory of denoting complexes that Russell put forward in his early phase. He ignored such ingredients of the sentence of natural language, representing it as meaning "for every x, if x is a dog, then for some y, y owns x" (more exactly, as "Whatever x may be, if x is a dog, then it is not the case that, whatever y may be, y does not own x"). This is surely not an analysis of the original sentence, but a translation of it into a different language. If it is an analysis of anything, it can only be an analysis of the thought expressed by the original sentence, or of its judgeable content, in the terminology Frege used in *Begriffsschrift*.

It is not at all clear, however, that Frege would have accepted this argument, or the dichotomy on which it is based. He says, for example, that the word "dog," as used in such a sentence, is being used predicatively, that is, as if it occurred as part of the predicate "is a dog." How can that be understood save as saying that the sentence should be understood as saying that everything, if it is a dog, has an owner? A thought is the sense of a sentence; an analysis of a thought is accordingly thereby an analysis of a sentence that expressed it. In his late article *"Der Gedanke"* ("Thoughts") of 1918, Frege says that what he is really interested in are thoughts, but that he can give instances of them only by means of sentences expressing them: he has therefore to give attention to language, despite the need to fight its misleading features. In many places he says that the composition of a thought out of its component parts by and large corresponds with the composition of the sentence that expresses it out of *its* parts. He also held that we human beings can grasp thoughts only as expressed linguistically or symbolically.

It is plain that the opposition between the analysis of thoughts and of sentences is an unreal one. It is true that much that Frege says, such as that a predicate must be well defined for every object as argument, is intended to apply not to natural language as it actually exists, but to a language adapted to science and to fully trustworthy deductive argument. Natural language was, in his view, in great measure defective: it failed to measure up to what a language ought to be. (Since many sentences of natural language are ambiguous, this can hardly be denied, even if Frege's requirements were too exigent.) Yet Frege always expressed the fundamental notions of his theory in application to linguistic expressions: sense and reference are always the sense and the reference of an expression. In the famous article "*Über Sinn und Bedeutung*" he engages in much discussion of matters strictly to do with natural language. In particular, the celebrated doctrine that within indirect speech, governed by such a verb as "believes," the words refer to what in other contexts are their sense, and the entire clause to the thought ordinarily expressed by the sentence following the conjunction "that," relates only to natural language, since no indirect speech is expressible in Frege's formal language or occurs in any proposition of mathematics.

In the masterpiece of his early period, the *Grundlagen der Arithmetik*, Frege wrote throughout as discussing the meanings of ordinary sentences, including mathematical ones. He is concerned to explain and analyze their meanings. Notions of content and meaning, object, concept, and relation are tools in this analysis; but there can be no sense in saying that he is concerned with the contents of sentences as opposed to the sentences whose contents they are. And indeed it is in the *Grundlagen* that the linguistic turn occurred for the first time in the history of philosophy. § 62 of the book opens with a question in Kantian style: "How, then, are numbers to be given to us, if we can have no idea or intuition of them?" The question is epistemological in the first instance—how can we know anything of the numbers? But it is also ontological— with what right can we hold that there are such things as numbers? Frege's first step, in answering the question, is to appeal to his context principle: only in the context of a sentence do words have meaning. He therefore directs attention to sentences in which terms for numbers occur. The question then becomes how such sentences are endowed with sense, and that is the topic of the ensuing inquiry. An epistemological and ontological question is to be answered by an account of the senses of certain sentences. There could not be any more perfect example of the linguistic turn.

11

GADAMER ON LANGUAGE

The rapid acceptance of the new logic, modern mathematical logic, came about with little direct influence from its founder, Frege. A major influence was the massive three-volume *Principia Mathematica* (1910–1913) of Bertrand Russell and Alfred Whitehead, the equivalent of Frege's *Grundgesetze*; it attempted to derive the whole of mathematics from logical first principles, in a formal system based on the ramified thoery of types. Russell had learned from Frege and from Giuseppe Peano, but others studied the *Principia* rather than the authors' forebears. An equally powerful influence in propagating the new logic was the work of the school of David Hilbert, particularly the textbook *Grundzüge der theoretischen Logik* (*Outlines of Theoretical Logic*, 1928) by Hilbert and Ackermann. The new logic had a profound influence on philosophers of the emerging analytic school.

Analytic philosophy has a twofold heritage: British, from the work of Bertrand Russell and G. E. Moore, both in revolt against the absolute idealism then prevalent in Britain; and Austrian, from Wittgenstein, who published his famous *Tractatus*

Logico-Philosophicus in 1922, and the Vienna Circle, which initiated the movement known as logical positivism. One member of the circle, Rudolf Carnap, had actually attended Frege's lectures; Moritz Schlick and Friedrich Waismann were both greatly influenced by Wittgenstein, on whom the formative influences had been Russell and Frege. Influenced by the positivism of Ernst Mach, the Vienna Circle was strongly empiricist, an orientation Frege would have greatly disliked. Its best known doctine was the senselessness of all metaphysics; almost equally celebrated was the thesis that the meaning of a sentence is the method of its verification. Nazism drove most members of the circle, and others of similar outlook, out of Austria, Germany, and Poland, mostly to the United States, while Wittgenstein worked in Cambridge. Analytic philosophy ceased to be Anglo-Austrian and became Anglo-American. In America it mingled with the native pragmatist tradition; much of the homegrown production of analytic philosophy, above all the work of W.V. O. Quine, took its inpiration, in large part by reaction, from the writing and teaching of Carnap. To England Alfred Ayer had brought back from Vienna the pure logical positivist doctrine. In Oxford, a more relaxed school, concerned to achieve exact descriptions of the everyday use of expressions of natural language, for a brief period presented itself as showing for the first time how philosophy ought to be practiced; this "ordinary language" school of philosophy was dominated by Gilbert Ryle and then by John Austin.

These various manifestations of analytic philosophy differed widely among themselves; but the orientation of all of them was determined by the linguistic turn. The study of language, whether systematic or piecemeal, was substituted for the study of thought. Many would have equated it with the study of thought, on the ground that we can think only in words. Wittgenstein's example of someone writing in pencil, breaking off to look at its point, shrugging, and resuming his work illustrates the falsity of this assumption: the writer clearly thinks, "The pencil is blunt; oh, well, it will do," but need not embody his thought in words, only in his actions. Yet the fundamental principle underlying the concentration on language was that an analysis of linguistic meaning is the best means—indeed the only effective means—for analyzing the thoughts we can express in language. Hence when, in the 1970s, the work of Frege began to be influential, the idea of a systematic theory of meaning assumed a prime importance. Quite recently, certain philosophers working within the analytic tradition have abandoned this principle and engaged upon a direct study of thought, independent of its linguistic expression. But in doing so, they remain indebted to an analysis of the structure of thoughts ultimately derived from Frege's theory of meaning.

It is of interest to compare with Frege's analysis of language the reflections on language of a philosopher outside the analytic tradition. In his book *Truth and Method* Hans-Georg Gadamer, the only philosopher so far to have celebrated the centenary of his own birth, devoted its last chapter to language. In it, he shows great interest in the concept of understanding. He explains that he is not concerned with the understanding of what another says that is directed at forming a view of the other's character or inner life, but only with understanding concerned with the truth or falsity of what the other says. Given Gadamer's great interest in art, it is surprising that he does not mention fiction in this context. When we read a novel or a verse epic such as "Beowulf" or "Orlando Furioso," it is essential for us to understand what we read, but we know that it does not purport to be true; yet we do not read to gain an insight into the soul of the author. Frege frequently cited fiction as a case in which we are concerned with the senses of the sentences, that is, the thoughts they express, but not with their truth values. But he himself insisted that thoughts are intimately connected with the notion of truth: to grasp a thought is to know what is required to determine it as true. Our understanding of a work of fiction consists in our knowing what it would be for it to be true, even though we are unconcerned with whether it *is* true, or take for granted that it is not.

Despite Gadamer's great interest in the concept of understanding, he manifests no interest in the correlative concept of meaning. This seems quite odd, since to understand a sentence is to know what it means. He more than once expresses antagonism toward what he calls "the philosophy of language," but he does not appear to mean by this what I or any other analytic philosopher would, but rather, comparative philology, whose foundation he ascribes to Wilhelm von Humboldt. He says that his concern is the opposite of Humboldt's: it is how, amid the varieties of different languages, "there is still the same unity of thought and speech, so that everything that has been transmitted in writing can be understood." Frege would say that Gadamer was interested in the thoughts expressed by language rather than in language itself; but it is plain that he does not consider thought possible without language.

Gadamer's unconcern with the concept of meaning shows that he has not been seized by the wonder from which a philosopher's interest in language would spring if he were to become what I should call a philosopher of language. How is it that words—sounds of a certain kind or marks on paper—mean anything? What is meaning? Two people are sitting talking to each other. They alternately emit sounds. They may be gossiping about a common acquaintance, making plans for a holiday they are taking together, arguing about politics, discussing the behavior of subatomic particles. How does it come about that, simply by making sounds of a particular kind, they manage to do these things? How does language work? It is to answer questions such as these that we attempt to devise a theory of meaning.

Because Gadamer is uninterested in the concept of meaning, he makes no proposal to explain how the meaning of a sentence derives from the meanings of the words composing it. This may seem surprising, since the concept of understanding, which does interest him, is correlative to that of meaning: to understand a sentence, it is necessary to have a tacit grasp of its structure, as is readily shown by the misunderstanding of a sentence that is ambiguous because it may be taken as having one structure or a different one. Not only that: Gadamer says nothing about the components of understanding. For Frege, to understand a sentence is to know the force attached to it, to grasp the thought it expresses, and to be aware of its coloring. Gadamer does not subdivide understanding in this or any alternative way: he works with a unitary notion of understanding. Frege always discussed sentences as the units of meaning. It may reasonably be objected that there is more to meaning than this. Understanding a speech or lecture, or a connected piece of dialogue, does not consist merely in understanding each of the sentences it comprises: otherwise the order of the sentences could be arbitrarily rearranged without loss, save that a little adjustment of pronouns and demonstratives referring back to what was previously mentioned would be needed. To understand a speech or connected text, it is necessary to know how the speaker or writer intends the sentences to be related to one another. Is something asserted as following from what went before, or as giving the reason for it? Is it said as exemplifying what was said previously, or as a concession, modifying its generality? Such relations between what is expressed by successive sentences are sometimes indicated explicitly by words such as "hence" or "admittedly" but often left implicit; a grasp of them is an essential ingredient of understanding. Gadamer is no more interested in this feature of understanding of an entire speech or piece of writing than in the components of the understanding of a single sentence. He takes the operation of linguistic understanding for granted: he is concerned only with its very general nature.

Gadamer rightly says that writing is a representation of spoken language; at least this is true of most existing systems of writing—

not only alphabetic and syllabic ones but also Chinese characters—although it is not true of Arabic or Roman numerals, or of mathematical and logical symbolism in general. "All writing claims that it can be awakened into spoken language," Gadamer says. He makes the evident point that, in contrast to speech, there is no extraneous aid to the interpretation of a written text. Unless we are conversing on the telephone, we are guided in understanding what someone says by his gestures and expression, and always by his intonation; we can also ask him to elucidate. Gadamer evidently considers speech as not only temporally but also theoretically prior to writing.

Gadamer insists that understanding involves interpretation. In this he would be roundly applauded by Davidson, for whom a hearer's understanding of a speaker consists in his interpreting the other's words; he most usually calls the hearer "the interpreter." For Gadamer, as for Davidson, an interpretation is alays expressible in words. He nvertheless says that "the interpretation that music or a play undergoes when it is performed is not basically different from the understanding of a text when you read it: understanding always includes interpretation." This is surely untrue. The reason a piece of music requires interpretation by the performer is that not every detail of the performace can be laid down in the musical score: selecting the attack and the tempo may be based on an estimate of the composer's intention or simply on what seems appropriate or expressive, but it is not at all like interpreting an ancient Chinese text or a paragraph from a modern French philosopher. To interpret such a text is to be able to say what it means, but a performer interprets a piece of music by playing it, and anything he said would be at best a guide to such an interpretation.

For Davidson, the understanding of what someone else says requires the hearer to interpret the speaker because he regards them as speaking different languages. That is, each has his own idiolect: the hearer must in his own idiolect interpret the speaker's idiolect. We can indeed, for any language that a speaker knows, divide its expressions, as used in particular ways, into three categories: those that the speaker knows and would so use himself; those that he understands when so used by others, but would not himself use in that way; and those that he does not know at all. Such a classification represents his idiolect when speaking that language. But to take an idiolect as the fundamental notion in explaining understanding within a theory of meaning is to overlook the imporatance of our having languages that are common to many: it is the common practice in using such a language that determines the meanings of its words and expressions. Gadamer does not adopt so extreme a view as Davidson; he speaks of different languages in the usual sense, while of course recognizing that they change over time. He nevertheless believes, presumably for reasons akin to those of Davidson, that interpretation is integral to all understanding, even the understanding of an utterance in a language common to speaker and hearer.

Gadamer believes that sometimes a difference in language reflects a difference in conceptual scheme. He does not labor the point; but, speaking of historians, he says that one of them may "take no account of the fact that the descriptive aptness of his chosen concepts . . . assimilates what is historically different to what is familiar, and thus, despite all objectivity, has already subordinated the alien being of the object to its own conceptual frame of reference" (p. 357). This appears to conflict with the views of Davidson, who rejects the notion of conceptual schemes altogether. We understand another, even an ancient writer from a different culture, by interpreting him. We can interpret him only in our own language, which embodies the range of concepts available to us. If what he says resists any such interpretation, then it is opaque to us: we are not in a position to attribute any meaning to his words, nor to credit him with having any conceptual scheme.

It is unclear whether there is here a genuine disagreement between Gadamer and Davidson. It is undeniable that someone may lack a concept that others have, and that we now have many concepts that no one had three hundred years ago. New concepts are continually introduced. They cannot always be defined in the existing language, but they can be explained by means of it; a study of how we acquire concepts, such as the concept of infinity, that could not even be expressed before their introduction would be highly illuminating. It is also undeniable that we can now recognize, of certain concepts that were used in some previous age, that they were incoherent or confused. Interpretation of a text requires, not necessarily that we should be able to *express* the concepts it invokes, but that we should be able, in our present language, to *explain* them; and this includes explaining what it was to have those concepts we now regard as confused. Interpretation does not make the heavy demand on the interpreter's stock of concepts that it contain all those invoked in the text (or piece of spoken discourse) that he is interpreting: it makes only the light demand that he be able to explain those concepts, or explain what it is to have them, in his own language. Only if it is impossible to give such an explanation is the interpreter justified in denying that the text has a genuine meaning and expresses no concepts, not even incoherent ones.

It is probable that Gadamer and Davidson could agree on this. Indeed, one passage by Davidson from the volume devoted to him in the *Library of Living Philosophers* (p. 308) suggests that he has a very restricted view of the range of concepts common to all who know a language:

Every natural language we know has expressive powers very similar to those of the most highly developed languages. These powers are: an underlying logical structure equivalent to the first-order predicate calculus with identity, an ontology of medium-sized objects' causal potentialities and a location in public space and time, ways of referring to the speaker and others, to places, to the past, to the present and future. Children get this far early. Once one has this core, one has a language, and it can be translated into any other. . . . The elements in anyone's language or repertoire of concepts that lie outside the shared core I think of as suburbs of the core.

This last metaphor is also to be found in Wittgenstein. As described, possession of such a central core allows great deviation in concepts that affect daily life. A person's identity determines what he owns, what he owes, who his spouse and relatives are, what rewards or punishments he is due. It would be consistent with commanding that central core that a society should have quite different criteria of personal identity from those generally customary. For instance, its members might make determinate identifications of children as reincarnations of deceased adults; another society might take certain rites of passage as the coming to be of a quite new individual. But perhaps Davidson intended our usual criteria of personal identity to be included in the central core. In any case, the different conceptual schemes of the historian and people of the earlier age that he was studying envisaged by Gadamer probably relate only to the "suburbs"; so there is no genuine clash between the two philosophers on this question.

Gadamer rightly calls attention, as Husserl had done before him, to the fusion of a word with its meaning in the mind of a speaker, particularly of a speaker who knows only one language and perhaps is unaware, or only dimly aware, that there are other languages. For such a speaker, the meaning of the word seems to be intrinsic to it, just as one who knows a particular alphabet, Roman, Greek, or Cyrillic, cannot see a letter save as having the associated sound. Trees, according to him, are called "trees" because they *are* trees. One of my daughters once took a job as a waitress. Two French girls at another waitress's table asked for "pommes frites." "What do they mean?" the waitress asked my daughter. "They mean 'chips,'" she answered. "Why don't they say so, then?" the other waitress replied.

It is nevertheless remarkable how easy it is to grasp that there are different languages. A child brought up to be bilingual does not utter macaronic sentences: he speaks in one language or the other.

Gadamer insists that the correct interpretation of a text is not a matter of divining the author's intention: "the horizon of understanding cannot be limited either by what the writer had originally in mind, or by the horizon of the person to whom the text was addressed," he says. This is a fashionable view, but unless it is applied very narrowly, it is wild. In general, to undertsand what someone said or wrote is to grasp what he meant by it. It is true that sometimes ideas may be latent in a text of which the writer was not clearly aware; but what he wrote is certainly not to be treated as a timeless *objet trouvé*, isolable from the context in which it was composed.

This prompts the question whether a speaker or writer is to be said to understand his own words, to know what he means by them. Again, there are rare instances in which it is correct to say that someone does not know what he is saying, or even that he does not mean anything at all. But generally, a speaker knows what he means, a writer understands what he has written. Now what does his understanding consist in? Not in an interpretation: what could such a self-interpretation look like? William Cowper said that God is his own interpreter to us, but no one can be his own interpreter to *himself*. No one needs to interpret himself to himself. In the *Philosophical Investigations* Wittgenstein famously said that "there is a way of grasping a rule which is not an interpretation" (§201). We may add, more generally, that there is always a way of understanding something that is not an interpretation.

There must be, on pain of infinite regress: since an interpretation is expressible in words, it too must be understood. A speaker's understanding of what he himself says is an understanding that is not an interpretatation. Moreover, a hearer's understanding of what another says is usually of just the same kind as the speaker's understanding of what he is saying. This does not apply when the hearer has an imperfect knowledge of the language the speaker is using, or when the speaker uses some words in a nonstandard way: in these cases interpretation is needed. But when speaker and hearer are conversing in a language they both know very well, they are engaging in a complex, shared practice that both have mastered: they no more need to interpret each other than a child playing Tic-tac-toe needs to interpret a move by his opponent. Gadamer and Davidson are both mistaken in believing that understanding always involves interpretation.

Gadamer devotes a section to Plato's Cratylus. On the opposition between assuming a natural agreement between word and object and a conventionalist explanation of how a word comes to have the meaning that it does, he comments that the question that is right presupposes that we already know what objects there are for our words to apply to. The comment implies that it is through language that we determine what are the objects we see the world as containing. This means, presumably, that it is we who choose what criteria of identity for objects of different sorts we shall use; but, as so often in this chapter, the thought is not pursued. Gadamer says that the Cratylus takes the first step toward what he calls "the modern instrumental theory of language." He plainly feels some distaste for this, and remarks that "The word is not just a sign. In a sense that is hard to grasp it is also something like an image." Its striking us as like an image is surely due to that fusion of word and meaning on which Gadamer had remarked earlier; but this psychological effect has no tendency to refute a conventionalist account of what confers meanings on the words of language.

Gadamer turns with relief to the Christian analogy between the scholastic account of human language and the theology of the Trinity, of which the second person is the Word. This very interesting discussion does not further our understanding of how human language works, because the scholastics were primarily concerned not with spoken or written language but with the *verbum cordis* or *verbum intellectus*, the language of the heart or of the mind. Gadamer rightly objects that "the 'language of reason' is not a special language": understanding spoken or written language does not consist in translating it into an inner language of thought. This would have been the place for Gadamer to develop an account of the relation between language and thought, but it is another line of inquiry that he does not here pursue.

In the penultimate section on language and concept formation, Gadamer declares that "language is not just one of man's possessions in the world, but on it depends the fact that man has a world at all." To have a world, he explains, is to have an attitude toward it: "this capacity is both the having a 'world' and the having of language." The concept of a world (*Welt*) is to be distinguished from the concept of an environment (*Umwelt*); animals have an environment, with which they can deal intelligently, but, being without language, do not have a world. Gadamer concludes his final section by declaring, "That which can be understood is language." It would be more accurate to say that whatever can be recognized as expressing a thought is language, and a gloss would then be needed to differentiate expression from indication and manifestation; many things that are not languages, such as somebody's reason for not attending the board meeting, can be understood.

The contrast between Frege's and Gadamer's approaches to language is stark. From Frege we get sharp, detailed, innovative analysis; from Gadmer, ruminations at a high level of generality. Which approach is found more illuminating is a matter of temperament. Some may feel like addressing to Frege the words William

Blake addressed to Aristotle: "it is but lost time to converse with you whose works are only Analytics" (*The Marriage of Heaven and Hell*). Others, myself included, will feel that Frege's systematic treatment helps them toward a solution of the problems that first aroused their wonderment far better than the more diffuse discussion of Gadamer. There is a space, and indeed a need, for philosophical discussion of high-level questions about language; but answers to such questions will be solidly based only if there is, or at least it is possible to construct, a credibly analytic account of how language works.

12

THE PARADOX OF ANALYSIS

G. E. Moore maintained that philosophers had erred in thinking it the task of philosophy either to refute certain propositions to which common sense would ordinarily assent, or to defend them against purported refutation. Such propositions were not, in his view, to be called in question. What was uncertain was the correct *analysis* of those propositions, and that was the proper task of philosophy. We could not sensibly doubt the truth of common-sense propositions, but without the help of philosophers, we could not say exactly what they mean.

Philosophy should thus consist in the analysis of concepts or of meanings. But the notion of analysis led to apparent paradox, which greatly preoccupied Moore and his colleagues. The outcome of conceptual analysis must be an evident analytic truth, incapable of giving us new information. A correct analysis should yield a definition faithful to the meaning of the defined term. There could not then be any doubt of its correctness, for if anyone understands two expressions, he must thereby know whether they have the same or different meanings. This left little for philosophy to do, if its task were to analyze concepts, and made it a mystery how there could be disputes in philosophy.

Frege's notes of 1914 for his lecture course on logic in mathematics show no interest in conceptual analysis. He distinguishes between constructive and analytic definitions. The former lay down how a new expression is to be used, or how the author intends to use an old one; the expression defined and that used to define it are then stipulated to have the same sense. An analytic definition aims to capture the sense of a term already in use. If successful, it will be immediately recognizable as such; if there is any doubt, this can be because we never had a clear grasp of the sense of the term we are trying to analyze. In this case, Frege recommends that we abandon the attempt at analysis; we should introduce a new term, stipulatively defined to have the sense given by our failed analytic definition. Frege was here raising a flag of surrender in the face of the paradox of analysis.

Yet conceptual analysis had lain at the heart of his attempt to provide foundations for arithmetic. He had proposed to show the truths of arithmetic to be analytic in the sense of being deducible by means of definitions from the fundamental laws of logic. In *Grundlagen* he wrote:

> Starting from these philosophical questions, we come upon the same demand as that which has independently arisen within the domain of mathematics itself: to prove the basic propositions of arithmetic with the utmost rigor, whenever this can be done. . . . If we now try to meet this demand, we very soon arrive at propositions a proof of which remains impossible so long as we do not succeed in analyzing the concepts that occur in them into simpler ones or in reducing them to what has greater generality.

The contructive part of Frege's *Grundlagen* contains a series of definitions of fundamental arithmetical terms. Such definitions must be intended as analytic ones. As Eva Picardi has written in her essay "Frege on Definitions and Logical Proof":

> Without the premises that definitions afford an analysis or reconstruction of the meaning of the arithmetical sentences which is somehow responsible to the meaning of these sentences as these are understood, the logicist idea of providing an analysis of the sense of arithmetical sentences by uncovering the grounds on which a justification for their assertion rests would be incomprehensible.

That is to say, Frege's definitions must be understood as aiming to capture the senses we attach to the arithmetical terms as we ordinarily use them; otherwise no proof of arithmetical propositions containing those terms would show those propositions, as we ordinarily understand them, to be analytically true.

It seems that, in the thirty years between the composition of *Grundlagen* and that of the lecture on logic in mathematics, Frege's views on definitions must have undergone a substantial change. In *Grundlagen* he had spoken of definitions as fruitful; as Eva Picardi has noted, he ceased thereafter to do so, and in the lecture notes he considers them as having psychological but not logical importance. In his review, published in 1894, of Husserl's *Philosophie der Arithmetik* of 1891, Frege offered a very weak criterion for the correctness of a definition:

> In this matter there appears a division between psychologistic logicians and mathematicians. The concern of the former is with the sense of the words and the ideas that they fail to distinguish from the sense. The mathematicians, by contrast, are concerned with the matter itself, that is, with the reference of the words. The objection [made by Husserl], that it is not the concept, but its extension, that gets defined,

is really directed against all mathematical definitions. For a mathematician the definition of a conic as the circumference of the intersection between a plane and the surface of a right cone is neither more correct nor more incorrect than its definition as a plane curve whose equation with respect to rectangular co-ordinates is of degree 2. His choosing either of these two definitions . . . will be based on convenience, regardless of the fact that these expressions neither have the same sense nor give rise to the same ideas.

The contention that all that is required of a definition is that it secure the correct reference for the defined term is preposterous; to derive a statement of arithmetic from fundamental laws of logic by means of such definitions would certainly not be enough to show it to be analytic in the sense intended in *Grundlagen*. In any case, the two definitions of "conic" cited by Frege are not merely coextensive: they are provably coextensive. Moreover, Frege shows no concern in his review of Husserl for what greatly concerned Husserl in his book, and had equally concerned Frege in *Grundlagen*: that an expression ought to be defined in terms of what is conceptually prior to it. That is, if notion A is defined in terms of notion B, then either notion B can plausibly be treated as a primitive notion neither needing nor admitting of definition, or it must be possible to define notion B in turn without reference to notion A.

Husserl had discovered the paradox of analysis. Frege, in his review of Husserl's book, shows himself blind to the paradox. Frege summarizes a form of objection to the definitions given in *Grundlagen*, used several times by Husserl, as follows:

If words and phrases refer to ideas, then, for any two of them, there is no other possibility than that they either designate the same idea or different ones. In the first case, to equate them by means of a definition will be pointless—"an obvious circle" [Husserl's own phrase]; in the other it will be incorrect. These are the two objections, of which the author regularly lodges one or the other. Even the sense is something that a definition is incapable of analyzing; for the analyzed sense is, as such, not the same as the original one. Either, with the word defined, I already clearly think everything that I think with the defining expression, and then we have the "obvious circle"; or the defining expression has a more richly articulated sense, so that with it I do not think the same as with that being defined, and hence the definition is incorrect.

Frege meant by "ideas" (*Vorstellungen*) mental images, sensory impressions, and the like; he was right to regard Husserl, who, when he wrote *Philosophie der Arithmetik*, had highly psychologistic views, as taking the propensity to arouse ideas, in this sense, as part of a word's meaning. But if we apply Husserl's argument to sense, it is evident that he had hit precisely on the paradox of analysis that later would so trouble Moore. Husserl's argument is a fork: either an analytic definition must be trivial because immediately obvious, or it is incorrect.

Of the many definitions Frege gave in his *Grundlagen*, and of those discussed by Husserl, we may choose as representative the celebrated definition of numerical equivalence. The concept is familiar not just to mathematicians but to everyone; and the definition purports to give an analysis of that concept. The definition was not in fact original with Frege but had been in currency among mathematicians for several years, as he acknowledged; Frege adopted it and gave it its most precise logical formulation. An answer to a question of the form, "How many . . . s are there?" may be definite or indefinite. The answer "A hundred and seven" is definite; the answer "between a hundred and a hundred and twenty" is indefinite. When, as Cantor did, we consider seriously

"How many?" questions as applied to things of which there are more than finitely many, we come to need a clarification of the concept of numerical (or cardinal) equivalence. Is "Infinitely many" to a "How many?" question a definite or an indefinite answer? Well, when does a response, say "Umpteen," to a "How many?" question answer it at all? Clearly when, whenever there are umpteen things of one kind, F, and there are just the same number of things of that kind as of another kind, G, it follows that there are umpteen things of kind G (or, as we may say for brevity, umpteen Gs). This leaves it open that "umpteen" might be an indefinite answer to the question. So what is required for it to be a definite answer? It will be definite if, whenever there are umpteen Fs, there will be just the same number of Gs if and only if there are umpteen Gs. By this criterion, Cantor showed, "Infinitely many" is only an indefinite answer to the question "How many?": there may be infinitely many Fs and infinitely many Gs, and yet not the same number of Fs as of Gs. There are, e.g., the same number of rational numbers as of integers, but there are not the same number of rational numbers as of real numbers.

To arrive at this result, it is necessary to know when it is true to say that there are the same number of things of one kind as of another. At first glance, the answer seems obvious: find out how many things of the one kind there are and how many of the other; if the result is the same in both cases, there are the same number of things of each kind; if the result is different, there are not. This is essentially Husserl's answer to the question when it is true to say that there are the same number of things of one kind as of another. But what is it to specify the number of things there are of a given kind? When there are only finitely many things of that kind, we know a method, at least in principle, of doing this: count them. (When there are too many, this method will be impossible in practice.) But if we are interested in the general case, when there may be infinitely many things of the given kind, this method may not be applicable even in theory. We may try the following explanation: to determine how many things there are of a certain kind is to find a definite answer to the question, "How many things of that kind are there?" But now, when we look back at our characterization of definite answers to "How many?" questions, we find that it relies on the notion of there being the same number of things of each of two kinds; and just that is what we were trying to explain. So our explanation is circular: we have neglected considerations of conceptual priority.

Given that our characterization of a definite answer to a "How many?" question was correct, we therefore need, in order to avoid the circularity, a definition of "There are the same number of things of one kind as of another" that does not require it to be said how many of either kind there are. It will be better to express "there are the same number of" differently, because that suggests the answer we have set aside; we may say "There are just as many" instead. The definition Frege adopted of "There are just as many Fs as Gs" was essentially this:

There is a one-one function ϕ that maps the Fs onto the Gs. A function ϕ is one-one if it has different values for different arguments. It maps the Fs on to the Gs if, for every x that is F, ϕ (x) is a G, and for every y that is G, there is an x that is F such that ϕ (x) is y. Frege points out that we can use this criterion in everyday situations to ascertain that there are just as many things of one kind as of another, without determining how many of either there are. Suppose that, at some stage of a ball, every girl is dancing with just one young man, and every young man is dancing with just one girl. Then there are evidently just as many girls as young men at the ball. This is because, in these circumstances, "partner of" is a one-one function that maps the girls onto the young men.

Does this definition give a true analysis of the expression "there are just as many"? Our first inclination is to say not: for surely we know perfectly well what it means to say, for example, that there are just as many small cakes on some dish as plates on the table without so much as having the concept of a one-one map. Ask any child what that means, and he will almost certainly answer, "If you count the cakes on the dish and count the plates on the table, you will get the same answer." Husserl agreed. He admitted in his book that the definition adopted by Frege "lays down *a necessary and sufficient condition*, in the logical sense, valid in all cases" for there to be just as many things of one kind as of another. But he objected that the possibility of a one-one mapping does not "constitute their *equinumerosity*, but only *guarantees* it." "To know that their numbers are equal does not in the least require knowing that it is possible" to map one to the other, and so "the one piece of knowledge is in no way identical with the other." Rather, despite his general qualms about analyzing any concept, he thinks that counting the things of one kind and of the other and coming to the same number in each case corresponds to what "just as many" *means*: "the simplest criterion for equality of number is just obtaining *the same number* when one counts the sets to be compared."

How decisive is Husserl's criticism? The most obvious weakness of the criterion he proposes is that it does not apply to the infinite case. But it may be retorted that our everyday understanding of "just as many" does not cover the infinite case either: if we want to treat of infinite totalities, we shall have to decide how we want to extend our notion of the number of members of a totality to them. Frege's first response is to observe that when, for example, we count the cakes on a dish and find that there are seventeen, what we have done is to map the cakes onto the number-words from "one" to "seventeen." This is evidently true. Primitive shepherds make notches on a tally stick to keep track of the number of sheep in the flock; our number-words provide us with a universal tally. But, granted the justice of Frege's observation, it may still be said that, in understanding the concept expressed by the phrase "just as many," we have no need of the *general* notion of a one-one map.

Does the victory in this dispute go to Husserl, then? Well, consider this case. A child has learned to count: he counts the cakes on a dish, meant for a party, and finds that there are seventeen of them. "Good!" says his mother, "then there will be just enough to go around," for there are sixteen children coming to the party, which, with her son, will make seventeen. What does "there are just enough to go around" mean? Clearly, it is a colloquial way of expressing that there is a one-one map of cakes on the dish onto children at the party. The mother is unconsciously relying on the theorem that, if there is a one-one map of cakes onto the number-words from "one" to "seventeen" and a one-one map of children onto the number-words from "one" to "seventeen," then there is a one-one map of cakes onto children. Yet what if the child does not understand his mother's statement, "There will be just enough to go around"? He asks, "What do you mean, Mother?" and when she answers, "There will be a cake for everybody," he asks, "Why?" or "How do you know?" She will be able quite quickly to explain and get him to see the point, but before he came to see this application of numerical statements such as "There are seventeen cakes," ought we to say that he fully understood such statements? He had learned to count, and could therefore know what was needed to make such a statement; he to that degree partly understood that form of words. And yet he had not grasped the most basic application of numerical statements, so we must allow his understanding of them to have been imperfect.

We do not use such an expression as "a one-one map" in everyday speech, but our use of such expressions as "just enough to go around" shows that we are in fact familiar with the concept it expresses, and associate it very closely with statements of number. The child who, when asked how one can tell whether there are just as many things of one kind as of another, answers in Husserl's way that you must count both and see if they come to the same total, can nevertheless easily be brought to agree that, by matching things of the first kind one to one with things of the second, you can find out that there are just as many of each without counting either. Frege actually defined the individual numbers by appeal, ultimately, to the notion expressed by "just as many." There is no strict necessity to do so: they can be defined without invoking numerical comparison. Yet we see from the example of the child who did not understand the notion "enough to go around" that he was far from having been absolutely wrong to define them as he did.

The paradox of analysis arises from the idea that anyone who grasps the sense of two expressions must be able, if those senses are the same, immediately to recognize that they are: there is therefore no need of reflection to see that a conceptual analysis is correct, if it is. Now indeed it must be possible for anyone who understands two synonymous expressions to come to recognize that their senses are identical; if it were not, no conceptual analysis could ever be established as correct. But this does not imply that it may not take some reflection, or even exposure to some argumentation, to bring us to that recognition. This is because, when we come to consider some concept, or the meaning of some expression, in a context when we are not in fact applying that concept or using that expression, we frequently overlook some connections that we automatically make when engaged in applying the concept or using the expression. The line between having the same sense and being demonstrably equivalent is not a sharp one. Certainly the latter notion is weaker than the former: there are undoubtedly cases in which a deductive proof is needed to show that two expressions whose senses are not at all the same are nevertheless coextensive. But there is no definite answer to the question how much reflection is allowable for a recognition that two expressions mean the same. Frege's terminology of "grasping a sense" misleads us into thinking that the process must be instantaneous, but mastering a concept or comprehending a form of words is a complex process, and we frequently do not get beyond a partial mastery or a partial comprehension. The understanding of an expression, the mastery of a concept, consists in a range of interconnected abilities, and one who has these abilities may well not have apprehended the connections between them. What someone grasps in practice need not always come overtly to mind when he is asked how to explain an expression, or even whether a given explanation is correct. That is why conceptual analysis can bring to light connections that we have failed to notice between different components of the complex linguistic practices in which we have become competent, and even abilities that we have failed to notice that we possess.

Because of the interconnections, it is often indeterminate whether a definition of one of a circle of related expressions is correct, or whether possession of a certain linguistic skill suffices to ascribe understanding of one such expression. A system of definitions parcels out the meanings of the expressions that form the circle, and it can be asked whether that system comprises all that it is collectively necessary to know in order to be said to understand all those expressions. But to the question whether each item should be allocated to this expression or to another, there need be no single correct answer.

For these reasons neither the task of conceptual analysis nor the recognition that it has been correctly executed is trivial, as Husserl and Moore feared that it might be. But, though not trivial, is it not to be classed as a mere empirical study? It unravels features of our linguistic practice of which we may not have been fully aware, and is that any more than the observation of an aspect of human behavior?

Would it really be disconcerting if the answer were that it is no more than that? Wittgenstein remarked that the task of the philosopher consisted in assembling reminders of things we already know, but do bear in mind when we are wrestling with philosophical perplexities. Yet it is not true, as Wittgenstein also asserted, that philosophy must leave everything as it is. Human languages are marvelous instruments for the expression of thoughts. Yet they are not perfect instruments, and the philosopher concerned to analyze our concepts has not only to describe but also, on occasion, to criticize. The most obvious defects of language, such as evident ambiguities, whether in the meanings of individual words or in the structure of sentences, do not need philosophers to detect or rectify; but there may also be ambiguities not easy to spot. There are concepts we do not know how to extend to cover new types of case; there are also concepts that may be revealed as confused by an attempt to analyze them. The most general description of serious defects of language is the following. There are two aspects to the application of a concept or deployment of a thought, or to the use of a sentence or a word. On the one hand is the condition that warrants us in applying the concept or in using the word, accepting the thought as true or making an assertion by uttering the sentence. On the other hand are the consequences of accepting the thought or endorsing the statement, both consequences to what further thoughts or statements we infer and consequences in our actions. In a language free of defect, there would be harmony between these two aspects. We ought to draw from a statement that we have accepted only those consequences that the condition that warrants its assertion entitles us to draw; conversely, we ought to have the right to draw all the consequences to which the condition that warrants the assertion of the statement entitles us. There is, however, no guarantee that a common linguistic practice, governed by general social conventions, will ensure such harmony. The most obvious examples of disharmony spring from prejudice and superstition. To a racially prejudiced employer, a man's race may count as a reason not to employ him; to a superstitious person, the fact that someone is coming downstairs is a reason for not going upstairs. In both cases the consequence drawn fails to match the grounds for the proposition from which it was drawn. These disharmonies are obvious; there surely are others only detectable by deep reflection. A philosopher engaged in conceptual analysis will come upon defects of language, and in particular covert disharmonies, that casual consideration must fail to detect, and he will perceive how they are to be corrected. Conceptual analysis is therefore not a matter solely of describing how things are with our conceptual system, but of criticizing and improving it: it is in part a creative enterprise.

13

THOUGHT AND LANGUAGE

Frege was earlier described as the first to make the linguistic turn, when, in the *Grundlagen*, he answered the question "How are numbers given to us?" by an investigation of the senses of sentences containing terms for numbers. But was it really *language* that he was interested in? The sentences he discussed were German sentences. Yet, when the *Grundlagen* is translated into English or Italian, the sentences he was inquiring into are also translated into English or Italian. Surely it was not the German sentences Frege was concerned with, but the *thoughts* they and their English and Italian counterparts express.

This would be an unjustified opposition. Frege says that he is concerned with the senses of sentences, and his inquiry is concerned with the senses of sentences. He is concerned with that aspect of language that renders it translatable. Languages are not like games. It makes no sense to ask what the equivalent of castling is in draughts; but it always makes sense to ask how to say such-and-such in any given language, and there will always be an answer, even if a somewhat qualified one. The reason it is often difficult, and sometimes next to impossible, to translate from one language into another is best explained in terms of Frege's distinction between sense and coloring. The sense of a sentence is constituted by what will determine it as true or as false; the sense of a sentence, considered as uttered by a particular speaker on a particular occasion, is what Frege called a "thought." The coloring of a sentence is what is conveyed by the way it is framed, insofar as this does not affect its truth or falsity. Our forms of expression convey our attitude to what we are speaking or writing of; they evoke associations and atmospheres, and indicate or hint at what is coming next or the relation we wish the hearer or reader to perceive as obtaining to what went before or what is coming next. All this belongs to coloring: it cannot affect whether what is said is true or false. The sense is what is left when we prescind from the coloring: it alone determines and is determined by the truth condition of the statement being made. The coloring of an expression in some language may not be precisely, or even imprecisely, matched by that of any expression with the same sense in some other language, which is why it may be next to impossible to translate exactly from one language to the other. But it is always possible to convey in language a thought expressed by a sentence in some other language, at least if we are allowed inelegant circumlocutions and, when necessary, some preliminary definitions or explanations. Given any condition whatever for the truth of a thought, expressible by a sentence of some one language, it must be possible to frame, in any other language, a sentence for whose truth the same condition obtains, even if, before framing it, a good deal of stage-setting, in the same language, is needed. Frege was interested in the *senses* of sentences, not in their coloring. We may express that by saying that he was interested in the thoughts the sentences express; but whatever he himself may sometimes have said, it is wrong to say that he was interested in thoughts *as opposed to* sentences. He was interested in sentences in virtue of their expressing thoughts; he had no means of displaying the structure of thoughts save by displaying the structure of sentences expressing them, although the structure of sentences of natural language might best be conveyed by rendering them in his symbolic notation.

But why should a *philosopher*, as opposed to a linguist, concern himself with language at all? It is in thought that we conceive of reality. The philosopher is concerned with the nature of reality, and hence with how we conceive of it. He must therefore occupy himself with the clarification of human thought. But what access has he to thoughts, and by what means, in addressing others, can he refer to them and explain how they are clarified? No other means presents itself save their linguistic expression. He can single out a thought by means of a sentence expressing it; he can analyze that thought by analyzing the structure of that sentence and the meanings of the words that compose it; he can clarify the thought by discussing the meaning of the sentence and what is required for it to be true. If the philosopher's only means of scrutinizing thoughts is through the examination of how they are expressed in language, then he must concern himself with language: with the sense of sentences, not primarily with their coloring, in Frege's terminology.

That was the reason for the linguistic turn. That is why Wittgenstein, for example, discusses language throughout his *Philosophical Investigations*, and also why that book may, with very little loss, be translated from German into English, so that the translation speaks of English sentences where the original spoke of German ones. Occasionally Wittgenstein shows himself interested in features of German that do not carry over to French or Italian, as when he speaks of the reactions of a German when he discovers that in French and Italian an adjective serving as complement to the copula agrees in gender with the subject, which it does not do in German. But for the most part, Wittgenstein, like Frege, is interested in the *senses* of the sentences he discusses, which is why his book can be translated.

But is it a mere accident, as it were, of the fact that we have language but not telepathy, that philosophers are obliged to give their attention to language? Well, *could* we have the thoughts we do if we had no language? The best way to answer this is to consider how far we can ascribe thoughts to creatures that have no language. As Wittgenstein remarked in the *Investigations*, a dog can be afraid that his master is going to beat him, but not that his master is going to beat him tomorrow. It seems that there are very simple thoughts that an animal can have, and that he cannot have slightly more complex ones. A better insight into the matter is obtained by elaborating an example of Frege's. On a particular route, a dog is liable to be attacked by other dogs. Sometimes just one hostile dog attacks him, sometimes several do. Our dog adopts the policy of standing his ground when opposed by just one hostile dog, but of retreating when opposed by more than one. This appears a conceivable course of events. We may naturally say, "The dog can tell when there is only one dog barring his path"; in some sense, this seems undeniable. But does the dog have the very same thought that one of us would have when thinking "There is just one dog barring my path"? To credit the dog with doing so would require us, as Frege says, to ascribe to him a grasp of the concept we express by means of the word "one"; we should then have to suppose that he apprehended what was in common between his being opposed by just one dog, burying just one bone, finding just one person in the house, and so on. Quite evidently, we have no ground for attributing any such conceptual achievement to him; indeed, no canine behavior is conceivable that would warrant the attribution. So the dog does *not* have the very thought by which we express the feature of the situation he has recognized. Conversely, we have no linguistic means of expressing just what it is he recognizes. Animals without language cannot have the very same thoughts as those we express in language. They have something that plays a similar role in their behavior to that which our grasp of thoughts plays in ours. We may say that they have "proto-thoughts," but the expression is no more than programmatic; to give a clear account of the phenomenon it covers would be very difficult indeed.

How, then, to give a clear account of the thoughts that human beings can have, once past infancy? The classical strategy of analytic philosophy has been to do so through a theory of meaning for language. An explanation of a thought expressible in language will proceed by explaining what it is for a sentence that expresses that thought to have the meaning that it does. Wittgenstein wrote that to understand a sentence is to understand a language. It would be impossible for a sentence to have the meaning that it has as a sentence of a particular language if there were no language for it to be in: if there were no other sentence or even expression belonging to the same language as it. Wittgenstein did not intend by his remark to espouse the extreme holist position that one cannot fully understand a sentence of, say, Italian if one does not know the entire Italian language (which of course nobody does). To understand a sentence requires one to understand a language to which it belongs, but this might be only a small fragment of the natural language in which it is framed. It is that fragment which must be understood if the given sentence is to be understood. This fragment could in principle constitute the whole of a language known to the members of some community, although in fact it does not. Such a language would be very deficient in expressive power, compared to any actual human language; all that matters is that it is not incoherent to imagine it as the whole language known by some group of people.

This fragment has two components. First, there are words that are conceptually prior to those occurring in the given sentence. A word X is conceptually prior to a word Y if it is impossible to understand Y unless you first understand X. Thus "mother" is conceptually prior to "father": you could not know what it was for someone to be someone else's father unless you first knew what it was for someone to be someone else's mother (I of course here intend an adult, not a small child's, understanding of these words). More exactly, the criterion should be that it is impossible to understand the word Y unless you have the concept expressed by X: one could come to understand "father" without knowing the word "mother" at all if one knew some other word that had the same meaning as "mother." The relation of conceptual priority determines a partial ordering of expressions of a language: into the fragmentary language that must be understood if the given sentence is to be understood must go all expressions that are conceptually prior to expressions occurring in the sentence, and all sentences that can be formed by means of them.

Second, there are words and expressions of the same level as those occurring in the given sentence, or more accurately, a sample selection of them. This follows from what Gareth Evans called the "generality constraint." A statement can be understood only as contrasted with another statement that might have been made. One can know what it is for something to be smooth only if one also knows what it would have been for it to be rough. One can know what it means to say, "There are many people here," only if one knows what it would have meant to say, "There are only a few people here." By these two means, any given sentence of a language will define a fragment of that language—not always a specific fragment, but a representative one—that must be understood if that sentence is to be understood. Acquiring a language is a cumulative process; it also requires certain ranges of expressions to be learned simultaneously.

Granted, then, that explaining what it is for any one given sentence to have the meaning that it does necessitates explaining the working of an entire language, even if a very small one, how is this to be accomplished? Words and expressions must be explained as contributing to the sense of sentences of which they form part; the sense of a sentence must be explained as determined by some feature of a statement made by the assertoric utterance of that sentence on its own in given circumstances. The most popular choice for this feature is the condition for that statement to be true in those circumstances; without endorsing this choice, let us assume it made by some theorist.

The theorist who thus bases his account of the senses of sentences on the conditions for the truth of statements made by means of them must connect the notion of truth with the practice of speaking the language. This must clearly be done by giving an account of the use of sentences to make assertions. One who makes a statement by the assertoric utterance of a sentence on its own thereby claims a warrant for representing that statement as true. Such a warrant may be secondhand: he may be basing his assertion on what another, whom he has no reason to think unreliable, has told him, or on what he has read. Such testimony can be trusted only if it is possible to trace it back to someone who had an original warrant for the assertion, that is, one not based on testimony. What is accepted as counting as an original warrant depends heavily upon the type of statement being made. This is a complicated matter that any comprehensive theory of meaning must survey; semantics is intertwined with epistemology.

The hearer may respond in any of several appropriate ways. He may object to the relevance of the assertion, asking, "What has that to do with it?" An explanation of this response requires an account of linguistic practice at a high level, encompassing the notion of a conversation and of a monologue discussion of a single topic. Again, the hearer may challenge or inquire after the speaker's warrant for the assertion, asking, "How do you know?" He may contradict the assertion, giving reasons for not thinking it true. The most common response will be for the hearer simply to accept the statement as true, altering his beliefs or his actions accordingly.

A theory of meaning, even for a very small language, is thus a complicated thing: it comprises a full description of the social practice of using the language. One that conforms to the pattern just described will have given an account of what it is for a speaker of the language to grasp the thoughts expressible by its sentences and the concepts expressible by its words and phrases. For, by explaining the condition for the truth of a statement made by the assertoric utterance of a given sentence of the language in particular circumstances, and attributing to the speakers a grasp of that condition, the theory will have explained the thought expressed by such an utterance, and have ascribed to the speakers a grasp of that thought. Likewise, by explaining the sense of the sentence as derived from the contributions made by its component words to determining that thought, and attributing to the speakers a knowledge of that contribution, it will have set out a condition for the speakers of the language to grasp the concepts expressed by those words and by phrases made from them. Obviously, it will give only a sufficient condition for grasping those thoughts and concepts; no one needs to know that particular language in order to grasp them. A more general condition for grasping a given thought will be to know the sense of an equivalent sentence in any other language; a more general condition for grasping the concept expressed by a given word of the language will be to understand a word that plays an analogous role in some other language.

Can even this be too restricted to constitute a *necessary* condition for grasping the thought or the concept? We have seen that a being without language cannot *in general* have just the same thoughts as one who has language. But may there not be some simple thoughts expressible in language and some simple concepts so expressible that such a being may have? Suppose that we allow that this may be so. On that supposition, can we not simplify our account of language, for instance by saying that the predicate "is circular" expresses the concept of circularity? To do this, we must explain, first, what it is for one without language, or not presupposed to have a language, to have the concept of circularity; and we must explain, second, what it is for a word to express a concept. We might explain a grasp of a concept, for instance that of circularity, as consisting in an ability to determine whether something exemplified it—whether it was circular, for example—and to manifest this recognition by differential behavior; thus to verify that something was circular, he might check that its diameter remained the same, whichever direction it was measured in. And we might explain a word's expressing the concept by its application: for instance, a predicate's expressing the concept of circularity by its being applicable to anything that exemplifies that concept. Or, again, an explanation of someone's grasp of the meaning of the word "five" would consist in ascribing to him a knowledge of the condition for the truth of statements of the forms "There are just five Ns," "There are fewer than five Ns," and "There are more than five Ns," where "N" represents some noun phrase. And an account of a grasp of the notion expressed by "five" by one devoid of language might attribute to him an ability to determine, of things of any particular kind, whether there were exactly five of them, fewer than five, or more than five, with differential behavior that signaled his recognition of one of these three different states of affairs. In giving a theory of meaning for a language, the appeal to a presumed prior grasp of the thoughts and concepts expressible in it has accomplished nothing whatever: it has merely transferred part of what would have been needed to explain an understanding of words of the language to an account of a grasp of the notions they express, considered as attributable to one who did not have, or yet have, the language in which to express them.

There is indeed an asymmetry in the foregoing accounts of a knowledge of meanings and of languageless grasp of concepts, as stated. A speaker of a language was credited with knowing what it is for something to be circular; one without language was required to know how to determine whether something was circular. But this difference has nothing to do with that between one who has language and one who does not: it arises only because we have selected different criteria for understanding a word and for grasping the concept it expresses. By adjusting one or the other, we can make the ability required for grasping the concept part of what is needed for an understanding of the word.

The supposition that a grasp of thoughts and concepts can be ascribed to one who has no language in which to express them is therefore completely idle. It makes the task of explaining the mastery of a language no simpler; it merely takes some components of such an explanation as part of a prior account of a grasp of the senses they express. Only to a very small degree is it plausible at all to suppose that a grasp of the thoughts that can be expressed in language could be attributed to one who as yet had no language; such a supposition effects no economy in an account of how language functions. That is why analytic philosophy has traditionally proceeded by replacing an attempted account of thought, formulated independently of its linguistic expression, by an account of the working of language.

14

REALISM

There is some historical evidence that there really was a noble called Roland who served under Charlemagne; but suppose that it is misleading, and that there was no such person as Roland. On this supposition, if someone says, "It was the Basques, not the Muslims, who attacked Roland," meaning to make a serious historical statement, what does the name "Roland" refer to as he uses it? Does it refer to a possible, though not actual, person? Are there possible but not actual people and objects? If there are not, then presumably "Roland," in that speaker's mouth, does not refer to anything. But in that case, how can what he said be meaningful? (This was the problem Russell posed in introducing his theory of descriptions.)

Do the theoretical entities of science, such as photons and quarks, really exist? Or are they merely hypothetical entities forming part of an intellectual mechanism for predicting the observable results of our laboratory experiments? The former option is usually termed "scientific realism," the latter "instrumentalism." Does the past, though it *has* passed, retain some kind of existence, and so render our statements about it true or false? Or are such statements made true or false, when they are either, only by our memories and the traces of past events to be found in the present? Are statements about the future determinately true or false, according to what will later happen? Or are statements in the future tense to be accounted true or false solely as they accord with our present intentions and present tendencies? When we speak of other people's emotions, mental images, and sensations, or of their intentions, attitudes, and beliefs, are we referring to what takes place within the medium of their minds, though indiscernible by anybody else? Or are we merely putting interpretations on their behavior, as the philosophical theory known as "behaviorism" would have it? Do mathematical statements refer to, and are they rendered true or false by, the constitutions of abstract structures of abstract objects related in particular ways? Or are mathematical structures and mathematical objects merely the product of the minds of mathematicians, which they inhabit rather than an abstract realm? The former option is known as platonism, the latter as constructivism. Is there truly an external world furnished with independently existing material objects—trees, rivers, mountains, insects, foxes, houses, roads, the sun, moon, and stars, the galaxies? Or, as the once very popular philosophical doctrine known as "phenomenalism" teaches, are material objects merely our constructs out of the impressions on our senses—visual, auditory, tactile, etc.—which we postulate in order to obtain a command of the regularities those impressions exhibit?

All the foregoing, highly traditional, philosophical questions are *metaphysical* ones: they are questions about what reality is composed of. Furthermore, they are all questions about one or another type of *realism*: about possible objects, about scientific theory, about the past and the future, about mental states and events, about mathematics, about material objects. Despite the differences in subject matter, there are strong similarities between the arguments used in support of and against the realist view in each of these cases. But how are we to resolve any of these disputes?

Each of the disputes concerns the interpretation of a certain class of statements; the realist maintains that these statements are to be taken at face value, while his opponent argues that what makes them true or false is not what the way they are framed would suggest, but something different. Are statements containing an empty proper name or other term about a possible object that it denotes, or are they to be judged true or false, or neither, by how things stand in the actual world? Are the theoretical statements of science about the theoretical entities to which they refer straightforwardly true or false, or are they to be judged according to their success in enabling us to predict observable outcomes of experiments? Do statements in the past tense relate to a realm of reality that has receded beyond our direct observation, or are they disguised ways of speaking about present memories and present traces? Do statements in the future tense related to a realm of reality that has not yet presented itself to us, or do they relate to present intentions and tendencies? Do statements about mental events and states describe conditions within worlds private to each one of us, or are they oblique ways of talking about our behavior? Do mathematical statements depict how things stand in a special, nonphysical, unchanging sector of reality, or are they about the constructions that mathematicians can carry out? Are statements about the external, physical world made true or false by the disposition of material objects existing independently of us and of our knowledge, or are they based entirely upon our sense impressions?

The answers to the metaphysical questions about this or that variety of realism thus turn on the correct interpretation of one or another class of statements. Metaphysics accordingly rests on semantics. Why is this? Wittgenstein opened his *Tractatus Logico-Philosophicus* by declaring that the world is the totality of facts, not of things. The composition of reality depends not just on what objects it contains but on what facts hold about them. Facts are true propositions; the fundamental notion of metaphysics is hence that of *truth*. Every semantic theory or theory of meaning needs, and must provide, a conception of truth. This is not to say that every semantic theory must use the notion of truth in assigning meanings to the sentences with which it deals. A classic truth-conditional semantics does so use it: it treats the meaning of a sentence as determined by the condition for an utterance of it to be true. But a possible-worlds semantics, used for sentences involving modalities such as necessity and possibility, does not so use the notion of being true *simpliciter*: it uses instead, as what we may call its central notion, that of being true in a possible world. The intuitionist semantics for mathematical statements does not use even such a relativized notion of truth as its central notion. It characterizes the understanding of a mathematical statement as an ability to recognize a construction as a proof of it. It therefore gives the meaning of such a statement by laying down what is to count as proving it, on the assumption that it is already known what constitutes a proof of any subsentences it may contain.

Nevertheless, a semantic theory needs a conception of truth, for two reasons. The first is to characterize valid inference. A deductive inference is valid if it transmits a certain desirable property of statements from premises to conclusion. Whatever property is chosen by a semantic theory to play this crucial role may be called the conception of truth proper to that theory.

To understand the second reason a semantic theory must incorporate a conception of truth, we need to distinguish two components of the meaning of a sentence. If a sentence is uttered assertorically on its own, a hearer who accepts the assertion as correct will come to know something about the world (or, if the assertion was *not* correct, he will suppose that he has learned something). The feature of the meaning of the sentence that determines what such a hearer will take himself to have learned may be called its *assertoric content.* The assertion was correct if the speaker was entitled to make it, or, at least, if such an entitlement was to be had; it was incorrect if no such entitlement existed. We may say that, in given circumstances, the assertoric content of a sentence was satisfied if a speaker would have been correct to make an assertion by uttering it on its own. A sentence is not always used on its own, however: it may be subjected to an operator, such as negation or a tense inflection, or it may form a subsentence of a complex sentence, such as a conditional or disjunction. The contribution the sentence makes to the meaning of another sentence formed in either of these ways is not determined solely by its assertoric content: we may call the component of its meaning that does determine this its *ingredient sense.* It is the ingredient sense of each sentence of the language that a semantic theory seeks to characterize. Two sentences may agree in assertoric content, yet differ in ingredient sense. Suppose that you are speaking to someone on the telephone, and he says either "It is raining here" or "It is raining where I am." It does not matter which: you will learn just the same, for the two sentences have the same assertoric content. But they do not have the same ingredient sense: if they are both subjected to the operator "always," we get two sentences—"It is always raining here" and "It is always raining where I am"—that have quite different meanings. We may stipulate a statement to be true if its assertoric content is satisfied. We need this notion in order to explain the significance of an assertion made by uttering a given sentence on its own. It is the same notion as that referred to when characterizing the validity of an inference: what we need to know is that we are entitled to assert the conclusion if we were entitled to assert the premises.

The conception of truth belonging to any one semantic theory will naturally be connected to whatever notion it takes as central in the sense explained above; different semantic theories will embody divergent conceptions of truth. For this reason the two-way conditionals formed according to the pattern "'Roland is dying' is true if and only if Roland is dying," which many analytic philosophers from Frege onward state to be constitutive of the notion of truth, do not hold good under all conceptions of truth. It follows from the definition of assertoric content that the assertoric content of "'Roland is dying' is true" must be the same as the assertoric content of "Roland is dying"; but in the biconditional sentence cited above, the sentence "Roland is dying" is a subsentence of a complex one, and hence its ingredient sense, rather than its assertoric content, is involved. The biconditional will imply all other biconditionals in which both sides of the original one have been subjected to the same operation, such as: "'Roland is dying' is not true if and only if Roland is not dying" and "'Roland is dying' was true if and only if Roland was dying"; but these will not hold good under all conceptions of truth.

The conception of truth that a semantic theory embodies is also its link to metaphysics: it is the point where a metaphysical view stems from a theory of meaning. Indeed, it is in semantic terms that we can most accurately say what constitutes a realistic interpretation of some given class of statements, and hence what constitutes realism concerning a given subject matter or sector of reality. A strict realist interpretation of a class of statements is one under which their semantics is taken as a classical truth-conditional one, with two truth values, *true* and *false*, with respect to which the principle of bivalence holds, and the statements are interpreted at face value in the sense that all expressions occurring in them having the apparent form of singular terms are construed as denoting objects within the domain (or universe of discourse, in the old-fashioned terminology). Bivalence is the principle that every statement is determinately either true or false, independently of our knowledge or capacity for knowledge. It is by construing all terms as having a denotation, even when there are no actual objects that they denote, that we arrive at realism concerning possible objects.

Russell's way of escaping from that variety of realism was to deny the status of genuine singular terms to definite descriptions and ordinary proper names; sentences containing them were to be so analyzed that no such singular terms remained.

Only slight deviations from strict realism result from minor modifications of this semantics, for instance by allowing statements to have one or more intermediate truth values, or to lack a truth value altogether, but still requiring that every statement have a determinate one of these truth values, or determinately lack one. This was Frege's way of avoiding realism about possible objects: he held that, if there was no such person as Roland, a sentence such as "Roland blew his horn" still expressed a thought, but one devoid of truth value. A modified realism of this kind obviously will not normally endorse bivalence; but we may require that, to be counted as a form of realism, it should endorse the law of excluded middle (excluded third). The law of excluded middle lays down that, for any statement "A" that has a truth value, the disjunctive statement "A or not A" must be true; the law may hold good even if the principle of bivalence fails. Consider, for example, a semantics for a mathematical theory, say set theory, in which the central notion is that of being true in a model of the theory; relatively to each model, the semantics is two-valued. The appropriate conception of truth will be that of being true in every model, that of falsity being false in every model. Plainly, if the mathematical theory has nonisomorphic models, the principle of bivalence will fail. But for every statement of the theory, the law of excluded middle will hold, since it will hold in every model, and therefore will be (absolutely) true.

Most theories devised by philosophers in order to resist one or another variety of realism—phenomenalism and behaviorism, for example—have been vitiated by two errors. First, the philosophers have attempted to *reduce* statements of the class they do not wish to interpret realistically to statements of some other kind, that is, to translate the one into the other. Such attempted translations have invariably failed. Second, they have continued to maintain a two-valued logic, and even the principle of bivalence, for the statements they have been trying to reduce to others, although all justification for it has evaporated. The first step in the reduction has usually been to translate statements for which there is no direct evidence of the favored kind into what are called "subjunctive conditionals." A subjunctive conditional is a statement of the form, "If it were the case that A, it would be the case that B"; let us say that the opposite of such a conditional is "If it were the case that A, it would be the case that not B." Thus the phenomenalist translates a statement about unobserved material objects into one of the form, "If a sighted observer were to occupy such-and-such a position, he would have such-and-such visual impressions," and its negation into the opposite of that conditional. The behaviorist translates a statement about an as yet unmanifested mental disposition into one of the form, "If the subject were in such-and-such a situation, he would behave in such-and-such a way," and, again, its negation into the opposite conditional. Under such translations, there is no warrant at all for maintaining bivalence for the original statement, since there is no general guarantee that one or the other of any pair of opposite subjunctive conditionals must hold good. We often look back upon some choice we have made at some stage in our lives, and wonder how things would have gone if we had made a different choice. But there need be no answer to this question; there may be no one conditional statement that gives the true answer.

Only one traditional theory repudiates a variety of realism, yet avoids these twin errors. That is intuitionism, the program instituted by L.E.J. Brouwer for recasting the whole of mathematics on the basis of a rejection of a realist interpretation of mathematical statements. Intuitionism makes no attempt to reduce mathematical statements to statements of some other kind. Nor does it explain their meanings, or those of the logical constants, in terms of the condition for a statement to *be* true, still less for it to possess some intermediate truth value. It explains them by laying down what is to be a proof of a statement. Thus a proof of "A or B" is to be an effective means of finding a proof of "A" or of "B"; and a proof of "If A, then B" is to be an effective means of transforming any proof of "A" into a proof of "B." Intuitionism can accept neither the law of excluded middle nor the principle of bivalence. A statement of the form "A or not A" can be asserted only when we have a means of either proving or refuting "A"; and if a statement is true only when a proof of it exists, and false only when a proof of its negation exists, there is no guarantee that an arbitrary statement will be either true or false. For this reason, the logic of intuitionistic mathematics—the system of principles determining what is to count as a valid deductive inference—differs from the classical logic of traditional mathematics. Intuitionistic mathematics provides a pattern for what a nonrealist or antirealist theory should be like.

Why should we want to construct an antirealist theory? What reason is there for repudiating realism? The reason is that a truth-conditional theory of meaning—by far the most popular among analytic philosophers—is incoherent. A theory of meaning must incorporate a theory of understanding, since understanding is integral to the practice of using a language: two people can converse in a language they both know only because each understands what the other says. If the meaning of a statement is given by the condition for it to be true, then an understanding of the statement must consist in a knowledge of that condition. But what will having such knowledge consist in? Many of the statements that we make are ones whose truth or falsity we could in principle decide if we took sufficient trouble. In the case of such a statement, a knowledge of the condition for it to be true may be taken to reside in a grasp of the means for deciding its truth value. Such a grasp need not be manifested by an ability to describe the procedure; it is sufficiently manifested by exhibiting the ability to carry it out. Language is a closely woven net; such an ability may reasonably and naturally be ascribed to someone who shows his ability to decide the truth of other statements containing the various words occurring in the statement with which we are concerned. But not every statement we make can in principle be so decided. Our understanding of a statement that is not so decidable consists in our ability to recognize whatever shows it to be true if we are presented with it, but we have no effective means, even in principle, of getting ourselves into a position in which we are able to recognize the statement as true or as false. There are various linguistic operations by means of which we can frame such statements. One is quantification over an infinite domain, as when we quantify over indefinite future time by means of words like "never," "eventually," and the like. Another is precisely the subjunctive conditional, which we use when we explain what it is for an object to have some property by saying that, if it were in such-and-such an environment, it would react in such-and-such a way; not only phenomenalists but also hard-headed operationalists resort to this form of explanation. Whether we ought also to add to these two operations reference to what is too remote in time and space for observation is a controversial question.

What, then, on a truth-conditional theory of meaning, does a speaker's understanding of a statement we have no effective means of deciding consist in? It cannot be simply his ability to recognize, whenever presented with it, whatever establishes the statement as true or as false. This shows only that he knows the condition for the statement to be recognizably true, and that for it to be recognizably false; what is it for him to know what it is for the statement to be true in those circumstances in which he cannot tell whether it is true or false? It is not possible to plead that there may be no circumstances in which either it or its negation is true, but cannot be recognized as such, for according to the principle of bivalence it must be either true or false. The speaker's knowledge of the condition for the truth of the statement can in such a case be explained only as his having an interior conception of that condition. It will be recalled that the whole strategy of analytical philosophy was to give a philosophical account of thought by giving a philosophical account of how language functions. But now it appears that a speaker's understanding of a sentence is to be explained as consisting in his grasp of a thought, namely his conception of the condition for its truth. The entire explanation has led around in a circle.

This argument does not relate to any particular class of statements, but is quite general: it controverts realism in its most general form. We therefore seek a general alternative. This alternative must be modeled on the intuitionistic theory of meaning of mathematical statements. The warrant for asserting a mathematical statement is a proof; that for asserting an arbitrary statement may be termed a "justification." We may accordingly use the name "justificationism" for this generalization of the intuitionistic theory of meaning to all discourse. On this account, the meaning of a statement is given by the most direct justification of it. Most statements cannot be used as reports of immediate observation, but can be established only by inference from what has been observed, so a justification will most usually have an inferential component; this illustrates the dependence of the meanings of some statements on those of other statements conceptually prior to them. It is important, however, that deductive inference does not enter only into direct justifications: it also supplies *indirect* justifications, since, as Frege maintained, it can advance our knowledge. On a justificationist theory of meaning, a deductive inference is valid if, given that the premises are justified, it provides an effective means of obtaining a direct justification of the conclusion: we do not then need to employ those means in order to be warranted in asserting the conclusion.

Justificationism bases its account of meaning on our use of language: what we primarily learn when we learn language is what counts as justifying our saying one thing or another. Our responses to what others say are based on this: we learn to treat statements made by others as if we had been justified in making them ourselves, and hence to make assertions derived from testimony. A justificationist theory of meaning thus stands much closer to a description of linguistic practice than does a realist, truth-conditional one. It cannot admit the principle of bivalence: for a statement we have no effective means of deciding, we have no guarantee that we shall arrive at a justification either of it or of its negation. The theory therefore cannot validate classical reasoning, but only reasoning in conformity with intuitionist logic. The resulting metaphysics is one that allows the existence of gaps in reality. A statement may not be either true or false, in which case there is no fact of the matter whether it is one or the other. But we can never identify any specific statement as neither true nor false: the possibility of hitting upon something that establishes it as true or that rules it out can never be closed off.

What conception of truth is proper to a justificationist theory? Clearly a statement is to be held true just in case there is a means, effective in principle, for finding a justification of it. But should this be taken to mean that there is a means available to *us* as we are now, with our particular position in time and space and our existing sensory and intellectual capacities? Or should it be more liberally interpreted to mean that there is, was, or will be such a means for a suitability equipped observer in the right position in space at the appropriate past, present, or future time? Various considerations pull us toward one, and other considerations toward the other, of these alternatives; large metaphysical consequences hang upon the choice. I shall not try to resolve the issue here, but leave any readers who are not unrepentant realists to resolve it for themselves.

RELATIVISM

In *Through the Looking-Glass* Lewis Carroll (C. L. Dodgson) narrated the following conversation, the first remark being made by Humpty Dumpty:

> ". . . that shows that there are three hundred and sixty-four days when you might get un-birthday presents—"
>
> "Certainly," said Alice.
>
> "And only one for birthday presents, you know. There's glory for you!"
>
> "I don't know what you mean by 'glory,'" Alice said.
>
> Humpty Dumpty smiled contemptuously. "Of course you don't—till I tell you. I meant 'there's a nice knock-down argument for you!'"
>
> "But 'glory' doesn't mean 'a nice knock-down argument,'" Alice objected.
>
> "When *I* use a word," Humpty Dumpty said in rather a scornful tone, "it means just what I choose it to mean—neither more nor less."

"The question is," said Alice, "whether you can make words mean so many different things."

"The question is," said Humpty Dumpty, "which is to be master—that's all."

It is, in Britain at least, a regular occurrence for professors of linguistics to write letters to the newspapers explaining why the view expressed by Alice, when she said, "But 'glory' doesn't mean a 'nice knock-down argument,'" is a piece of ignorant superstition. Words don't have meanings in *themselves*, they superciliously explain; they have them only because speakers bestow those meanings on them. That is one of the ways language changes, they continue; speakers endow words with new meanings. In arguing this, such experts in linguistics reason as if a word's meaning, in the mouth of any speaker, were a property that could as readily be inspected as the speaker's pronunciation or accent.

Of course, a word does not have a meaning "in itself," but in virtue of being a word in a particular language. I can of course announce that I propose to use a word in a particular way; but, that aside, it is none too easy to endow a word with a meaning, for example to comply with Wittgenstein's instruction to say, "It is terribly cold today," and mean, "It is gloriously hot today." The deliberate oddity of the instruction is illustrated in another passage from Wittgenstein (*Investigations*, § 665):

Imagine someone pointing to his cheek with an expression of pain and saying "abracadabra!"—We ask "What do you mean?" And he answers "I meant toothache."—You at once think to yourself: How can one "mean toothache" by that word? Or what did it mean to mean pain by that word?

A word has what meaning it has, not in virtue of being endowed with that meaning by a mental act of the speaker, but in virtue of being governed by rules for its use that hold good for speakers of the language to which it belongs. Experts in linguistics, of the type mentioned above, overlook the paradoxical nature of language. There is no authority to enforce the rules that govern it; they hold only as part of a common practice. For this reason, the rules may be broken and the practice change. But, if there were at any time no prevailing rules, there would be no right or wrong to what anyone said, and hence no meaning would attach to it. Mistakes are of two kinds: errors of fact and misuses of language. We can often discern what someone intended to say when it differs from what the words he uttered meant. Someone says, "The marriage between X and Y was consummated in the cathedral." We do not judge he was using "consummated" as if it meant "celebrated" by inspecting the meaning it bore as he uttered it; we judge that partly by the improbability of what he actually said, partly by the similarity of sound between "consummate" and "celebrate." If many speakers repeatedly confused the two words, one might cease to bear the meaning that it now has: the mistake would have become the rule. The rules of a language rest on general agreement among its speakers.

It is important to our linguistic practice that we are conscious of the words we use and those others use. It is possible to remember the content of what someone said but not the words he used. Suppose it was always like this for current speech: when someone spoke to us, we apprehended the thought he was expressing, but heard him speaking only as we sometimes hear something being said in the next room, without being able to discern the words. This would not be telepathy: the thought we apprehended would not be that which the speaker intended to convey, but that expressed by the words he used. In such a case, we should be able to correct what a speaker said, as not agreeing with the facts, but not misuses of words, since we should not be conscious of the words. The language of people for whom utterances thus only subliminally conveyed the speakers' thoughts would be far more stable than actual human languages.

It is a very natural thing to think of our sensations as absolutely private to us. Someone who has never studied philosophy at all may quite spontaneously ask, "How do I know whether what we both agree in calling 'red' does not look to you as what I should call 'blue'?" If this is a genuine possibility, then we have two different uses of color words. In one use, the public use, whether something is to be called "red" or not depends on public agreement: if every normally sighted person—everyone who is not blind or color-blind—concurs in calling it "red," or whatever is the word for "red" in his language, then it is red. But, on this very natural theory, such agreement, and therefore the whole public use of a color word, rests on its private use. Each individual applies the word "red" when he addresses another person because he recognizes his own visual impression as that he associates with the word "red." Different people may associate different visual impressions with the word: this association, which is private to each, governs that person's private use of that color word.

Similarly for all the senses. According to this theory—which the unphilosophical will not call a "theory" but just an obvious fact—we make this double use of all the words we employ to characterize sounds, smells, tastes, how things feel to the touch, and our personal sensations, such as aches and itches. The private meanings attached to these words by each of us are meanings in his own private language. It is a language that only he can understand, because those meanings are given by associating the various words with private sensations, which others do not and cannot experience.

Wittgenstein set his face against this conception that a word can be given a meaning in a private language by a private ostensive definition, that is, by an inner mental act whereby the subject directs his attention upon some sensation of his, labels it with a name, and later uses this name to himself whenever he recognizes that sensation as occurring again. If a word is to have meaning, there must be a correct way of using it or of applying it; and if it can be used correctly, it can be used incorrectly also. If my private name for a certain sensation is to have a meaning, my subsequent use of it must be correct or incorrect. It will be correct if I apply it to the same sensation, incorrect if I apply it to a different one. "But," Wittgenstien says, "in the present case I have no criterion of correctness. One would like to say: whatever is going to seem correct to me is correct. And that only means that here we cannot talk about 'correct'" (*Philosophical Investigations*, § 258).

For the use of a word to be right or wrong, it must belong to what Wittgenstein calls a "practice." In using the word, we are obeying a rule governing its use; and, Wittgenstein says, "'obeying a rule' is a practice. And to think one is obeying a rule is not to obey a rule. Hence it is not possible to obey a rule 'privately': otherwise thinking one was obeying a rule would be the same thing as obeying it" (§ 202). But the question now arises what constitutes a practice. The most obvious examples are those in which many people engage, such as the use of money, or giving presents on birthdays, or obeying traffic signals. But can there be a practice one person invents, and in which only that person engages? For there to be a right and wrong in the execution of the practice, it must be possible in principle for other people to discern the intended regularity in that practice, and hence to judge whether on a given occasion it has been carried out correctly: in that sense it must be public, even though it is not a common practice. Would it be possible, for example, for someone to have a language that was private, not in the sense that only he could understand it, but in the sense that only he knew it and hence only he understood it? For there to be a right and wrong in the use of the words of that language, it must be a language that others could come to understand, if they took the trouble, and hence judge when it was being used correctly and when incorrectly. But is there any absurdity in the idea that a genuine language might exist that was in fact only ever known to one human being?

On reflection, it is the stricter interpretation of the notion of a practice that fits our case. The user of a language must not only be right or wrong in what he says, as this may be judged by an external observer who makes no contact with him; he must be able to tell when he is right and when he is wrong. If he has no way of telling, then he will judge to be right whatever seems to him to be right; for him, whatever seems to be right *will* be right. Such a speaker will be unable to make a distinction between what is subjectively correct and what is objectively so; he will not have the concept of an objective error, either of fact or of usage. No one can have a language save as a member of a society that has the common practice of using that language.

Clearly, meaning is relative to a language and thus, in view of the foregoing argument, of a linguistic community; but can the truth of statements, and therefore also of beliefs, likewise be said to be so relative? There is no difficulty about an individual's having a mistaken belief of his own: the community will be able to apprise him of his mistake. But what if the members of an entire community are agreed that some statement is true: must it then not be true for them? For example, it was at one time universally agreed that the sun moves around the earth: was it not therefore true for the people living at that time that the sun moved around the earth? If so, where does that leave us who are living now? It seems to follow that anything on which we are unanimously agreed can be true only for us. There can then be no absolute truth.

More exactly, only those statements that contain an explicit relativization can be true absolutely. Strictly, we must qualify the statement "The earth moves around the sun" by inserting "For us" at the beginning; but we do not need to relativize once more the resulting statement, by saying, e.g., "It is true for us that it is true for us that the earth moves around the sun," for that would generate an absurd infinite regress. Now no perplexity arises from the fact that some form of words was once universally agreed to express a truth and is now universally agreed to express a falsehood, if it can be shown that some of the words have changed their meanings, or that their former meanings were incoherent, and that we have now rectified this. But this is implausible for the statement "The earth moves around the sun." How then are we to explain the change save by saying that what was once true is no longer true?

Someone who knows the meaning of a statement must be able to recognize evidence for its truth when he is presented with it. He must also be able to distinguish conclusive from defeasible evidence. If the people of former times took themselves to have conclusive evidence that the sun goes around the earth, then, unless they changed the meanings of their words, they could not admit anything as counterevidence against the truth of this proposition. In that case, we may indeed say that those words expressed a proposition that was true according to the meanings they assigned to them; but there is no ground to say that the very same proposition is false for us. But if the people of former times took themselves merely to have very strong evidence that fell short of being conclusive, there is no ground for saying that the proposition was true for them; they merely wrongly thought that it was true. It was simply a proposition for which they believed that they had strong evidence, but the meaning they attached to a sentence expressing that proposition allowed the possibility of counterevidence, which Galileo later brought to light. Indeed, they might have been brought to see that their evidence was weak; when someone said to Wittgenstein that it was natural to think that the sun goes around the earth because it looks as though it does, he retorted with the question previously quoted, "And how would it look if it looked as if the earth rotated on its axis?" The thesis of the relativity of truth is no more than a confusion engendered by a vivid awareness of the variations in the cultures of different times and places, and in the concepts then and there employed.

THE FUTURE OF PHILOSOPHY

In his article "The Four Phases of Philosophy" (*The Monist* 83 [2000]: 68–88), Peter Simons gives an elegant classification of various models of the history of philosophy:

> The most obvious and simplistic is the cumulative progress model: Philosophy progresses like science by cumulative achievement. . . . The cumulative progress model is, as Brentano pointed out . . . , too obviously falsified by the various setbacks, dark ages and regressive phases in philosophy to command assent. Philosophy is, says Brentano, more like the fine arts than the sciences in having degenerative periods. . . .
>
> More subtle is the dialectical progress model of Hegel: philosophy, though generally, progresses by setting up oppositions which are subverted but preserved at the next level. This allows for controversy, indeed requires it, but in Hegel's hands it too readily became teleologically loaded, moulding a

place in advance for Hegel's own system as the apotheosis of philosophy. . . .

The opposite of progress models are golden age models. A golden age model will claim that philosophy reached its zenith at some point (the golden age) in the past, only to have suffered a fall . . . from this height to a state of decadence or backwardness. A modern golden age model is that of Heidegger, for whom the pre-Socratics with their untrammeled concern with Being form the golden age. As Heidegger's case suggests, a usual concomitant of a golden age model is an analysis of the stages of decay from the original enlightened state, coupled with a recipe for reattaining that enlightenment, usually at the hands of the proponent of the model. . . .

More specific in their choice of good philosophy are Enlightened One models. An Enlightened One model takes some individual philosopher to have achieved a state of greatest philosophical enlightenment, never achieved before or since. . . . There are as many Enlightened One models as there are schools of epigone, but the most adulated Enlightened Ones in the history of philosophy have been Plato, Aristotle and Kant. . . . In our day the most prominent Enlightened One is Wittgenstein, but others in this century have been Bergson, Whitehead, Heidegger and Derrida. . . . The difficulty with Enlightened One models is that they have no general recipe for philosophical excellence beyond that of emulating the Master. . . .

There have been numerous brave new world models. In these, it is claimed that some new method or discovery gives us a completely new access to philosophical truth in a way which has never been given before: Now For the Very First Time we can sweep away the misconceptions of millennia of blind groping. The modern period has been especially susceptible to this kind of model. We have Descartes's method of doubt, Spinoza's axiomatic metaphysics, Leibniz's combinatorics, Hume's Newtonian analysis of human nature and Kant's critical philosophy. Closer to the present we have Brentano's descriptive psychology, Husserl's phenomenology, Meinong's object theory, Moore's conceptual analysis, the Vienna Circle's logico-linguistic analysis and Oxford ordinary-language philosophy. Brave new world models fulfill two desiderata for a subject which has made uncertain progress in two and a half millennia. They offer an account of why things have taken so long to get going properly (the proper method was lacking), and they present philosophy with a new justification for its existence, should there be those that doubt its credentials on its track record (up until now things were not so good, but *from now on, trust us, things are going to get better*). . . .

Examples of both the Enlightened One and the brave new world models are very familiar to me. Some followers of Wittgenstein take the attitude that he was the only one to understand how philosophy ought to be done, and that the writings of all other philosophers are concentrated nonsense; and during the brief dominance in Oxford of the "ordinary language" school there were many to proclaim that they were at last in possession of the right method in philosophy.

Simons criticizes all these models of the history of philosophy for failing to take account of the qualitative rise and fall of philosophy in different epochs. For this reason he prefers Brentano's cyclical model. According to this, philosophy repeatedly undergoes a cycle of four phases, which represent a steady decline: theoretical-natural; practical-popular; skeptical; and dogmatic-mystical. In the first of these philosophy is pursued as pure theory for its own sake. In the second, practical considerations predominate over theoretical; ethics and political thought override metaphysical and epistemological concerns. The skeptical phase needs no explanation; in the fourth mysticism competes with empty formulas and word games. Brentano recognized three such cycles as already having run their course—ancient, medieval, and modern. The decadent fourth phase of the modern cycle was represented by German idealism—Fichte, Schelling, and Hegel. But each fourth phase engenders the beginning of the first phase of a new cycle, which, as Simons says, Brentano saw himself as spearheading.

Simons regards Brentano's cyclical model as historically illuminating, and even constructs some (not very convincing) minicycles in the history of particular philosophical movements: for instance, Frege, Russell, and Moore as representing the first phase of analytic philosophy, James and Dewey the second, Wittgenstein and Quine the third, and Rorty the fourth; or Brentano and Husserl the first phase, Heidegger the second, Sartre the third, and Derrida the fourth of a rival tradition. But he complains that Brentano's cycles fit the general history of Western philosophy imperfectly, and that his explanation of the mechanisms leading from one phase to the next and from one cycle to the next are sketchy. He ends with no definite model to put in its place.

The major defect of Brentano's cyclical model is neither of those cited by Simons. It is that it overlooks the fact that philosophy is a sector in the quest for truth, or, more accurately, a search for a clearer understanding of the truths we already know. It thus allows no place for progress in philosophy; and if philosophy makes no progress, it is not worth wasting any time on. Philosophy cannot be compared with the fine arts without depreciating it. A cyclical theory of the history of art or of poetry would not depreciate those arts, because they do not aim at getting anywhere; if such a theory fitted the facts, it would just explain why art or poetry was of a higher quality at certain times than at others. But philosophy does have a goal; it can be pursued only in the belief that steps are being taken toward that goal. The sciences progress, if not in a perfectly straight line, then in a curve or zigzag that deviates only slightly from one. What is wrong with Simons's cumulative progress model is not that it postulates progress in philosophy, but that it represents that progress as being made in a nearly straight line. Rather, the path toward the goal of philosophy—any path that we can take—is a meandering one that twists and turns upon itself. At a given stage, the only way to proceed any further along this path may be to go quite a long way in a direction opposite to that in which the goal lies; to go in that direction may be the only way to improve our chance of eventually reaching the goal. On Brentano's model, however, philosophy does not make any progress toward its ultimate goal, either in a straight line or along a winding path: it simply goes in circles.

Where, then, is philosophy likely to go in the near future? Well, probably someone will put forward a brilliant and far-reaching idea that will fire the enthusiasm of a great many philosophers and eventually become an accepted instrument in the practice of the subject. Since I cannot tell what that idea will be, any predictions I make are likely to be falsified. But if this does not happen, some guesses seem probable. Plainly, the gravest obstacle to communal progress in philosophy has been the gulf that has opened between different traditions. Even Japanese philosophy departments are split between analytic philosophers, Heideggerians, Hegelians, and so on. Anyone who has read this book thus far will know that I believe it was analytic philosophy that took the most fruitful path: the study of language, both of how it works in general and of its particular features, has been far more fruitful than phenomenological intuition of essences, since as Wittgenstein remarked, "Essence is expressed by grammar" (*Investigations*, § 371). The prospects for a reconciliation between analytic philosophy and the hermeneutic and phenomenological traditions are better than they were forty years ago. There are analytical philosophers working in France and Spain, though very isolated from their colleagues of other persuasions; but in Italy, Germany, and the Netherlands an interest in the analytic tradition has become far more widespread, while those firmly attached to that tradition have studied and commented on Husserl and even Heidegger. The best point of contact between philosophers of divergent traditions surely lies in the philosophy of mind.

Scientists and philosophers have both become obsessed with the concept of consciousness. As previously remarked, experimental psychologists tend to view it as epiphenomenon; this is intrinsically absurd and due to a mechanistic interpretation of the human mind as a sort of metaphor for the human brain. Philosophers can obviously contribute much to this problem, or cluster of problems; and it is also the most likely area in which philosophers belonging to different traditions can cooperate. There is thus some hope that, in the coming decades, the gulf between divergent philosophical traditions may gradually be bridged.

If the scientism so prevalent within present-day American philosophy is intensified, a breach may open up between analytic philosophy as practiced in the United States and as practiced in Britain and continental Europe. This in itself may help to bring about a rapprochement between European philosophers of different traditions. The greatest lack, however, is of philosophers equipped to handle questions arising from modern physics; very few know anything like enough physics to be able to do so. This is a serious defect, because modern physical theories impinge profoundly upon deep metaphysical questions it is the business of philosophy to answer. We may hope that some philosophers may become sufficiently aware of this lack to acquire a knowledge of physics adequate for them both to integrate it with their treatment of metaphysical problems and to convey to philosophical colleagues who know less physics what they are talking about.

In this book I have deliberately highlighted those problems for which there is hope that a solution will soon be forthcoming, and that are to my mind the most urgent. I hope that work in analytical philosophy may bring about an agreed resolution of the dispute between realism and what I earlier named "justification," and, in particular, the question whether classical logic can be justified, or whether the logic used in intuitionistic mathematics is the "right" one generally. Collaboration between analytic philosophers and those of other traditions may bring about a resolution of the relation between language and thought. Is thought possible for a being without language? Even if it is, is a theory of linguistic meaning the best strategy for uncovering the structure of thought? And will it be possible to agree that the doctrine of the relativity of truth is a degenerate distortion of our welcome new sensitivity to cultural difference and our correct perception of the social character of language and thus of thought?

Finally, can philosophy settle what is surely the most important question of all, whether there are rational grounds for believing in the existence of God? There seems to me every reason to think that it can, and will even do so in the lifetimes of our great-grandchildren. My own belief is that it can be resolved positively; indeed, as a Catholic, I am committed to that belief. I have indicated earlier the lines on which I should argue for there being an omniscient God, whose knowledge constituted truth and who thereby was the Creator. Perhaps it can be deduced from the moral law, or from its absoluteness, that God has a will for us; certainly, since moral laws are not regularities like scientific laws, we have no right to talk of the moral law unless we posit a lawgiver. I do not know, however, how to argue that God has a will in general, so that it makes sense to ask for his purpose in what he does. Presumably beings who could think but not act—thinking trees—would have intelligence but no will; but how should one argue concerning a being for whom there is no distinction between thinking and acting? An omniscient being will need no reasons for believing as he does; must he have reasons for acting as he does, if acting and believing are for him one and the same? At present most Western philosophers do not believe in God, although the reverse was true up to 150 years ago. The only convincing argument that God cannot be shown to exist would show that he does not exist; from an intuitionist standpoint, these are the same thing. Conversely, the only convincing argument that God can be shown to exist would show that he does. That is not to say that, if the question were resolved negatively, all believing philosophers would instantly become atheists, or that, if it were resolved positively, all disbelieving philosophers would instantly become theists: no philosophical argument is ever compelling to that degree. Doubtless the proof or disproof of God's existence would rest on some premises that could be disputed, intelligibly even if not reasonably.